The LANGUAGE
OF LOVE

AN ANTHOLOGY *of* AUSTRALIAN
LOVE LETTERS, POETRY AND PROSE

The LANGUAGE OF LOVE

AN ANTHOLOGY of AUSTRALIAN LOVE LETTERS, POETRY AND PROSE

edited by

PAMELA ALLARDICE

Angus&Robertson
An imprint of HarperCollins*Publishers*

*Photographs, illustrations and documents reprinted
by arrangement with the copyright holders.
CollinsAngus&Robertson Publishers would be pleased
to hear from those copyright holders they were
unable to contact before publication.*

AN ANGUS & ROBERTSON BOOK
An imprint of HarperCollinsPublishers

*First published in Australia in 1991 by
CollinsAngus&Robertson Publishers Pty Limited (ACN 009 913 517)
A division of HarperCollinsPublishers (Australia) Pty Limited
4 Eden Park, 31 Waterloo Road, North Ryde, NSW 2113, Australia*

*HarperCollinsPublishers (New Zealand) Limited
31 View Road, Glenfield, Auckland 10, New Zealand*

*HarperCollinsPublishers Limited
77–85 Fulham Palace Road, London W6 8JB, United Kingdom*

Copyright © Pamela Allardice 1991

*National Library of Australia
Cataloguing-in-Publication data:*

*The language of love : an anthology of Australian love
letters, poetry and prose.*

*Bibliography.
ISBN 0 207 16895 4.*

*I. Love-letters. 2. Love poetry, Australian. 3. Love
stories, Australian. 4. Australian letters. I. Allardice,
Pamela, 1958–*
A820.8354

*Typeset in 12 pt Perpetua by Midlands Typesetters, Maryborough, Victoria.
Printed by Griffin Press, South Australia.*
5 4 3 2 1
95 94 93 92 91

INTRODUCTION

Distance and separation have long been a major part of Australian life, so it is not surprising that they feature prominently in our poetry, prose and fiction, as well as in private letters and diaries.

The colonials and convicts who first landed on Australian shores in 1788 often wrote to their families and loved ones of the loneliness and isolation of this vast continent. They expressed their feelings openly and at great length, as there was little chance of ever seeing their loved ones again. Letters often took up to two years to reach their destinations and some never arrived as ships were sometimes wrecked on their journeys home.

Campfire yarns also provide a record of tales of love about early settlers. These yarns played a significant role in the lives of the outback pioneers, miners and squatters as shown in the works of Henry Lawson, A. B. 'Banjo' Paterson and Arthur Hoey Davis (Steele Rudd). The songs and ballads of the bushrangers also lament the loss of the loved ones and lengthy separations.

Public stories from the oral tradition of the dreaming together with the works of the contemporary poets such as Oodgeroo Noonuccal give us a glimpse of traditional Australian Aboriginal relationships.

With the advent of modern technologies such as aeroplanes and telecommunications, the problems of distance and isolation no longer feature so prominently in the Australian psyche, but the tradition of writing about love and romance has continued in our literature.

The anthology is chronologically divided into three centuries, with each author's work occurring in the particular century to which it is appropriate. This makes it easier for the reader to locate particular writers or periods of interest.

The division begins with the 1700s and includes a letter by Captain William Bligh. His sadness at being parted from his wife typifies the isolation experienced by the early colonials. In the 1800s, the colony is more developed and new relationships between the settlers are being formed; E.W. Cole advertises for a prospective wife in the local Sydney newspaper. By the 1900s, many of the old traditions are lost in the freer speech of the new century. Australia is now exploring a series of possible identities and senses of freedom, and these possibilities are reflected in the love prose and poetry of this century.

*For Gregory, my husband,
sweetheart and best mate.*

Australian, Love Letters, Poetry and Prose

Excerpts from the journal and letters of Lieutenant Ralph Clark, whilst travelling to and stationed in New South Wales from 1787 to 1792, bear testimony to the love and affection he felt for his wife in England, Betsey Alicia:

SUNDAY THE 9 DECEMBER 1787

Dreamt that I was with my beloved Alicia and I thought that I put my hand in her breast—dear Sweet dream it was honey to my Soul although in a dream to be with You my adorable woman—I wish to dream of You and to be [with] You every night—how I long to be with you again believe me Betsey I will never goe from you again—this being Sunday kist your pictour my tender wife the mother of our dear Boy as usual on this day—I could not help saying to myself this morning when I was looking on it how good the Almighty has been to me to give So Beautiful So good So Vertious a Woman to wife as you are Betsey—I want word to praise your Vertious your are Surly ane Angle and not a Woman—Read the lessons and Spalms for the day—had no observation to day—thick nasty weather by the wind is fair thank God—went by the Log last 24 hours 148 miles—our consorts about a mile a head of use—thank heaven no sick on board—the Young lams and Piggs all well—3oClock PM. it blows and rain very hard—gave the seamen a bottle of Rum for the[y] are very wett and cold and a glas wont doe them any harm . . .

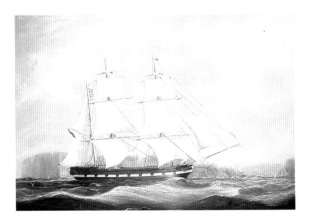

Unfortunately, the Clark family met a sad end: Betsey Alicia died after giving birth to their second child; Ralph Senior was killed in action in 1794 (fighting the French in Haiti) and probably died without knowing Betsey's fate; while young Ralphie, on the same ship as his father, died of yellow fever. The following is an excerpt from Clark's last letter to Betsey:

MAY 8 1794
MY EVER DEAR BELOVED ALICIA

As I expect the packet every day to call here for our letters on her way home, I have Sit again down to write you my ever dear beloved wife a few lines and to acquaint all that my soul most fondly doats on, that our dear and tenderly beloved Son and myself are both in perfect good health— . . . I wish that I could Say that my happiness was as great as my health is good—I assure you that it is not, for I am very much distressed on your Account my Alicia—indeed my beloved woman it is not possible for me to describe how unhappy I am at this Instant and have been for these some time past for fear any thing has happened to your health, or welfare my Betsey—indeed Betsey you cannot have a greater wish than I have to see and be with you at the time of your delivery—but I trust in god long before this you have been Safely brought to bed and that you my Alicia in whome all my Soul most tenderly doats on is by this time quite recovered and that also our dear beloved infant is in perfect good health—god what would I give to know but that happiness I am not able yet to know but must remain in the dreadfull suspence for a month longer . . .

I never was So much pleased with any letter in my life as the one dated the 23 of November where in you say that you never loved me So much as at the moment you then was writing—be assured my dearest Love I never will give reason to make you alter that love from me—I must leave room for Ralph to sign his name otherwise you will be unhappy—adieu now my dearest Love—compt. to every body m[y kin?]dred, god protect you my dear Alicia and my beloved child give it ten thousand kisses for me and I will repay you ten fold on my return—adieu my love take care of yourself and you will oblige your affectd.

HUSBAND, FRIEND AND LOVER
RALPH CLARK

My Dear Father has not left me any more room than to say God Bless You my Dear and best of Mothers prays your own Affectioned Son

RALPH STUART CLARK

The following, written by an unidentified hand, appears on the back of this last letter:

poor Mrs Clark was delivred of a dead Child herself Survived but a few hours—this was written Some days after her death—

EARLY PORTRAITS OF THE PURITANICAL REVEREND SAMUEL MARSDEN SHOW A HEAVY-CHESTED MAN WITH DARK BROWS AND A VERY SOMBRE EXPRESSION. EVEN THE OCCASION OF HIS COURTSHIP OF ELIZABETH FRISTAN DID NOT MERIT FRIVOLITY ON HIS PART. IN A LETTER TO HER HE EXPRESSED HIS BELIEF THAT GOD WISHED HIM TO JOURNEY AMONGST THE HEATHEN CONVICTS OF AUSTRALIA AND ASKED:

Dear Betsy . . . will you go along with me? Are you willing to take up your Cross and share my pleasures and my Pains? If, upon considering this subject you can answer in the affirmative and say I am willing, then my Heart (as far as it is proper that I should give it to the Creature) and all I have are yours . . . [I will be] happy in the enjoyment of [you] more than any other.

THE PAIR WERE MARRIED IN 1793 AND, SHORTLY AFTERWARDS, DEPARTED FOR THE ANTIPODES BRIMFUL OF EVANGELICAL ENTHUSIASM.

The popular impression of Captain William Bligh is of an arrogant, cold man. He is less known as a devoted husband and father, yet, immediately following the mutiny on his ship, the Bounty, his first instinct was to write to his 'Dear, Dear Betsy' and reassure his family of his welfare, as this excerpt from the transcript of his letter indicates:

COUPANG IN TIMOR
AUGT 19TH 1789

MY DEAR DEAR BETSY

I am now in a part of the world that I never expected, it is however a place that has afforded me relief and saved my life, and I have the happyness to assure you I am now in perfect health . . . What an emotion does my heart and soul feel that I have once more an opportunity of writing to you and my little Angels, and particularly as you have all been so near losing the best of Friends—when you would have had no person to have regarded you as I do, and you must have spent the remainder of your days without knowing what was become of me, or what would have been still worse, to have known I had been starved to Death at Sea or destroyed by Indians. All these dreadful circumstances I have combated with success and in the most extraordinary manner that ever happened, never dispairing from the first moment of my disaster but that I should overcome all my difficulties.

    Know then my own Dear Betsy, I have lost the Bounty . . . I know how shocked you will be at this affair but I request of you my Dear

Betsy to think nothing of it all is now past and we will again looked forward to future happyness. Nothing but true consciousness as an officer that I have done well could support me. I cannot write to Your Uncle or anyone, but my publick letters, therefore tell them all that they will find my character respectable and honor untarnished. I have saved my pursing Books so that all my profits hitherto will take place and all will be well. Give my blessing to my Dear Harriet, my Dear Mary, My Dear Betsy and to my Dear little stranger and tell them I shall soon be home. Remember to your Father and Annie Campbell and Mrs C and give affectionate respects to your Uncle and family. To You my love I give all that an affectionate Husband can give—Love, Respect and all that is or ever will be in the power of your ever affectionate Friend and Husband Wm Bligh.

If Ann Flinders hadn't taken her bonnet off one day in 1801 she would probably have voyaged to Australia with her husband, Matthew. He had installed his wife of three months in the captain's cabin of the Investigator, *hoping to present officials with her presence as a* fait accompli *once the ship had sailed. However, the commissioners of the Admiralty noticed her bonnet during their inspection and she had to disembark. Flinders was desperate without his wife, writing: 'I am just as awkward without thee as one half of a pair of scissors without its fellow.' Many such letters followed, for the pair were not reunited for nearly ten years.*

Ann's longed for letters were described by Matthew as the most important 'epochs' in his life, adding: 'I sigh for them as the best desired of blessings.' So affectionate and adoring were they, in fact, that he chided her gently:

. . . If I could laugh at the effusion of thy tenderness, it would be to see the idolatrous language thou frequently usest to me. Thou makest me an Idol and then worshippest it and, like some of the inhabitants of the East, thou also bestowest a little castigation occasionally, just to let the ugly deity know the value of thy devotion. Mindest thou not, my dearest love, that I shall be spoiled by thy endearing flatteries? I fear it, and yet can hardly part with one, so dear to me is thy affection in whatever way expressed . . .

Matthew wrote of their love in impassioned terms, likening his wife to:

. . . a vine whose twining arms when turned from round the limb lie prostrate, broken, life scarcely left enough to keep the withered leaf from falling off . . . Happy letter! Happy seal! [This letter] will be received by thee with joy, perhaps receive a kiss. O that I were freed from the bond of my parole, and could as easily be transported to thee. Still, my beloved, entertain hope. Misfortunes must sometimes have an end and what happiness will be ours when they shall cease . . .

DASHING SHIP'S SURGEON GEORGE BASS SWEPT ELIZABETH WATERHOUSE OFF HER FEET AND MARRIED HER—MINUS PARENTAL CONSENT ON EITHER SIDE—IN 1800. ALTHOUGH TAKEN BY SURPRISE, ELIZABETH'S PARENTS WELCOMED BASS INTO THEIR FAMILY AND THEY LIVED TOGETHER HAPPILY FOR THREE MONTHS, THE ONLY TASTE OF MARRIED LIFE THEY WERE TO KNOW BEFORE BASS DEPARTED ON A SEA VOYAGE. ONE OF HIS LAST LETTERS POIGNANTLY REFERS TO THE LOVELY ISLAND GIRLS HE HAD SEEN, BUT WHO ONLY MADE HIM LONG MORE FOR HIS WIFE:

My beloved wife . . . [I] do most sincerely lament that we are so far asunder . . . The next voyage I have [you] must make with me, for I shall badly pass it without you . . . I would joke . . . upon the attractive charms of Tahiti females but they have been so much belied in their beauty that [you] might think me attracted in good earnest. However, there is nothing to fear here.

BASS AND HIS SHIP WERE NEVER SEEN AGAIN, ALTHOUGH ELIZABETH REMAINED DESPERATELY HOPEFUL OF HIS RETURN UNTIL HER DEATH IN 1824.

When we are reunited thou wilt be to me not only a beloved wife, but my most dear and intimate friend . . . If we find failings, we will look upon them with kindness and compassion and in each other's merits we will take pride and delight to dwell upon them; Thus we will realise, as far as may be, the happiness of heaven on earth.

Governor Lachlan Macquarie dearly loved the bride of his youth, Jane Jarvis, as the entry describing his wedding night shows:

SEPTEMBER 8 1793

I handed Mrs Morley to her chair and saw her off; then undressed as quick as possible and flew on the wings of love to my dearest of women, to finally crown my measure of happiness and bliss! My felicity and delight, on this joyous and fortunate night, can only be conceived— but impossible to describe! Suffice it to say—no Benedict was ever happier, or better pleased with his lot and good fortune, in the choice of a Wife!

ON THE CONVICT WOMAN:

For the first of her virtues,
Was beauty you see,
And the hundred and second
Was chastity.

ANON
1800s

Jane died when Macquarie was serving in India, and the broken-hearted man swore he would never take another woman to that country. He was eventually to marry Elizabeth Campbell in 1805, but kept his promise by refusing to allow her to travel to India with him. Elizabeth accepted his suit and accompanied her husband to Australia, helping to bring many substantial improvements to the colony. Again, Macquarie recorded the details of his more mature, but nonetheless very fond, courtship in his journal:

MARCH 26. TUESDAY!!!

After very mature and deliberate consideration and reflection on all the consequences of so important a step, I took the opportunity this forenoon of waiting on Miss Elizabeth Henrietta Campbell . . . Finding her alone, I made a full avowal to her of my sentiments, and of my sincere love and ardent affections for her; explaining fully to her at the same time, previous to her giving me any answer to this declaration . . . the utter impossibility of our immediate union, nor until after my return from India . . . Miss Campbell heard all I had to say with the kindest and most good-natured attention; and then, to my infinite joy and delight, with a degree of noble candour and delicate liberal frankness, peculiar to herself, declared a most flattering return of the sentiments I had avowed . . . and kindly consented *to be mine* under all the untoward circumstances that opposed our mutual wishes for an immediate union;—and her readiness in yielding to the unavoidable delay of the happy event had endeared her to me more than ever and increased the high and exalted opinion already held of her virtue, refined delicacy and most excellent judgement and sound understanding. We discoursed a long time on this very interesting and delicate subject, and after perfectly explaining our wishes and sentiments to each other, we embraced affectionately.

'HELL HATH NO FURY LIKE A WOMAN SCORNED . . . '

BUSHRANGER MICHAEL HOWE WOULD HAVE DONE WELL TO HAVE KNOWN HIS SHAKESPEARE. IN 1814 HE KIDNAPPED AN ABORIGINAL 'WIFE', BLACK MARY, DESCRIBING HER AS 'A BROAD-FACED GIRL WITH FLASHING BROWN EYES AND WHITE TEETH—A FULL-BOSOMED AND BEAUTIFULLY BUILT SAVAGE'. BOTH TALL AND CLOTHED, ROBINSON CRUSOE STYLE, IN KANGAROO SKINS AND FEATHERS, THE PAIR WERE THE TALK OF HOBART. CHASED ONE DAY BY TROOPERS, BLACK MARY FELL AND HOWE CURSED HER FOR SLOWING THEIR PROGRESS. HE ANGRILY TURNED ON HER AND SHOT HER, POINT BLANK, WITH HIS PISTOL. HOWE FLED, BUT BLACK MARY LIVED TO TELL THE TROOPERS WHERE HER CALLOUS LOVER WAS HIDING. .

GIFTS

'I will bring you love,' said the young lover,
'A glad light to dance in your dark eye.
Pendants I will bring of the white bone,
And gay parrot feathers to deck your hair.'

But she only shook her head.

'I will put a child in your arms,' he said.
'Will be a great headman, great rain-maker.
I will make remembered songs about you
That all the tribes in all the wandering camps
Will sing for ever.'

But she was not impressed.

'I will bring you the still moonlight of the lagoon
And steal for you the singing of all the birds;
I will bring down the stars of heaven to you,
And put the bright rainbow into your hand.'

'No,' she said, 'bring me tree-grubs.'

OODGEROO OF THE TRIBE NOONUCCAL
(FORMERLY KATH WALKER)

The success of John Macarthur's merino wool-based dynasty was in no small part due to the hard work and determination of his wife, Elizabeth. He was exiled to England in 1812 for his part in the insurrection against Bligh and, for many years, the administration of her husband's estates fell to Elizabeth. During that time Macarthur's letters evidence the burgeoning respect and admiration he felt for his once 'timid and irresolute bride':

In the midst of all my difficulties I feel that I have the greatest reason to be thankful to God that your good sense enabled you to resist the temptation of coming to England, had it been so—into what an abyss of misery would you and my beloved Children have been plunged—dearest best beloved woman, how great are my obligations to you! . . .

I find it impossible to repress the pride which I feel in having to boast of such a pattern for wives and Mothers as my own . . . I do not urge you to patience, or entreat you to exercise your fortitude—because I know you will—you have done so to a degree that excites the admiration of all who have heard of your conduct, and will ensure the eternal gratitude of me and your children . . .

It will be the study of my life to requite you for all that you have suffered on my account . . . Believe me, my Elizabeth, the period of separation from you has been an almost uninterrupted scene of indescribable wretchedness . . . Practise, my beloved Elizabeth, yet a little longer the admirable fortitude that has enabled you for so many years to sustain such a train of afflictions and cheer your heart with the anticipation that the end of a stormy life may yet be passed in security, happiness and pease.

Some convicts fared well on their arrival in Australia and begged the authorities to allow their wives to join them in the new land. One convict, Josiah Godbyr, wrote to his 'dearest Rebecker' [sic] in 1815 of the life they could lead together in New South Wales:

I am as Comfortable as Posable in my sittewation but my Dear I could like to have you with mee and I should be happy . . .

I have said befoore my Dear Wife what would I give to here from you they say that absence and Length of Time will whare the thoughts of one another from our minds but my Dear Wife if I could but wonse moore Injoy your Company all the Powers on Earth should not Part us O my Deare To Think that we have lived To Gether so maney years and The Tourn a Sunder at Last it all moost Destracts me when I think of it my dear . . .

I am verry well of for a prisoner Government man to one Master Dixson a marchant and milnor Hee hath a Larg mill gose by a Steam Enguine I Dress flour and Seven pounds of Beef or Poark and Seven shillings that is my weeks allowance and a very good one for a Prisoner I have my Lodgins and Cloaths To find out of it but I have . . . as good Lodgins as any in the Town . . . my Dear . . . to have you with Mee and be Happy . . .

The Female Factory, Sydney's first women's prison, contained a tough bunch of inmates; however, given the scarcity of suitable women in the colony, a regular 'marriage market' was conducted there. Prout and Feely recorded:

The officer-in-charge would make a short speech: 'This young feller wants a wife. Any of you lasses who wants a chance to make a respectable woman of herself now has her chance. Step forward and let young Lochinvar here choose for himself!'

The wife-seeker would then toss his neckerchief at the feet of one of the women, and if she picked it up the 'proposal' was considered to have been accepted. Despite its resemblance to a cattle sale, this primitive system resulted in many happy marriages as these women worked alongside their husbands to build the colony.

THE LASS IN THE FEMALE FACTORY

ANONYMOUS

The Currency Lads may all fill their glasses
And drink the health of the Currency Lasses,
But the lass I adore, the lass for me,
Is the lass in the Female Factory.

O! Molly's her name and her name is Molly,
Although she was tried by the name of Polly;
She was tried and sent for death at Newry,
But the judge was bribed and so were the jury.

She got 'death recorded' in Newry town
For stealing her mistress's watch and gown;
Her little boy Paddy can tell you a tale,
His father was turnkey at Newry jail.

The first time I saw the comely lass
Was at Parramatta, going to Mass;
Says I: 'I'll marry you now in an hour.'
Says she: 'Well, go and fetch Father Power.'

But I got into trouble that very same night!
Being drunk in the street I got into a fight;
A constable seized me—I gave him a box—
And was put in the watch-house and then in the stocks.

O! It's very unaisy as I remember
To sit in the stocks in the month of December,
With the north wind so hot, and the hot sun right over.
O! Sure and it's no place at all for a lover!

'It's worse than the treadmill,' says I, 'Mr Dunn,
To sit here all day in the heat of the sun.'

'Either that or a dollar,' says he, 'for your folly'—
But if I had a dollar I'd drink it with Molly.

But now I am out again, early and late,
I sigh and I cry at the Factory gate.
'O! Mrs Reordan, late Mrs Farson,
O! Won't you let Molly come out very soon?'

'Is it Molly McGuigan!' says she to me.
'Is it now?' says I, for I know'd it was she.
'Is it her you mean that was put in the stocks
For beating her mistress, Mrs Cox?'

'O! yes, and it is, madam, pray let me in,
I have brought her a half-pint of Cooper's best gin.
She likes it as well as she likes her own mother,
O! Now let me in, madam, I am her brother.'

So the Currency lads may fill their glasses
And drink the health of the Currency lasses,
But the lass I adore, the lass for me,
Is the lass in the Female Factory.

Thomas Braidwood Wilson, a surgeon in the British Royal Navy, married Jane Thompson in 1826 and accepted repeated postings on convict transports to Australia and Tasmania over the next ten years, after which they both emigrated. Jane became quite angered over the long separations. Indeed, one home visit that lasted only ten days prompted this apologetic letter:

[I] . . . have scarcely as much [money] left as will buy your muff, which I herewith send you. Would to God I could give you more—you blame me wrongfully my sweetest Missie when you say I have behaved badly to you. Indeed I have exerted myself to the utmost & what a sacrifice of my own happiness to part so soon from you!—but duty necessarily has no love. Soon soon, my love, will the deep and stormy sea roll between us. My heart is too full to write—the tears are now following each other in quick succession down my weather worn cheeks. Be assured that my love, regard & affection for you are undiminished—if possible increased.

It pains me, that you think I have acted unkindly towards you. I know I do not deserve such censure & if I were to die next minute, my heart would be sorry on that account.

My inability & not my [will?] has been the cause of the privations you have experienced. But my sweet girl, another year elapsed & then we shall live happily and contentedly together . . . Farewell and believe me to be Your most faithful, most affectionate but miserable husband . . . kiss our little Mary . . . The pilot is leaving now as the wind is blowing fair—adieu & again adieu . . . I have written till the last moment— while you are reading this I shall be far down channel.

Given the formal society of the time few early settlers equated romantic love with marriage, hoping, instead, that these feelings would follow with time. Charles Sturt, for example, was a shy and introspective man, and paid only perfunctory attention to Charlotte Greene during their courtship. In a letter to Governor Darling about a month before their marriage in 1834, Sturt described his wife-to-be:

I had intended leaving England about the middle of last month, but a singular train of circumstances has arisen to prevent my doing so, and you will be surprised to hear that I am on the verge of marriage, having determined to sacrifice ambition at the shrine of domestic tranquillity and to exchange a restless disposition for one of quietude.

I know not that of myself I should ever have thought of such a measure; but it has been so strongly urged upon me that I have in a measure been obliged to give way—not one letter have I received from N.S. Wales in reply to my own, intimating my intention to returning to Sydney, but it contained the advice 'marry before you leave England'.

The Lady to whom I am about to be united has neither youth nor beauty to recommend, but if the most pleasing manners and the gentlest disposition, extreme firmness of mind and acquirements of no common order can weigh in the scale against such fleeting powers or render the softer sex estimable in our eyes, I have not been inconsistent in the choice I have made or built my hopes of domestic happiness on slight ground.

Beloved by all who know her and long known to my own family, Miss Greene is one to whom I could pay in advance the strongest tribute of confidence and esteem, nor can I doubt that she will make me a most affectionate wife and be to me a cheerful companion.

Despite its somewhat stilted beginning, the marriage appears to have flourished and Sturt's letters to his wife during his overland trip to Adelaide were filled with longing and concern:

Would to God I were in Adelaide, but why record my feelings and my sorrows in these pages. I can make even them my friends in this desert on which to unbosom myself. Could I have foreseen the tedious length of this journey I had never left my home. Time is flying on his iron wing, cruel and unrelenting time, and Oh I would not be from home much longer. Who have befriended my beloved wife during my absence? My heart shall be thine for ever. Does she give her husband credit for affection, or hope that he thinks of her, as I live she is never absent from me waking or sleeping. I have seen her palpable to touch as if she had been present . . .

THE NAME 'KISSING POINT' WAS GIVEN TO MANY SCENIC SPOTS FAVOURED BY COURTING COUPLES IN EARLY AUSTRALIA. THE KISSING POINT OFF PARRAMATTA ROAD WAS A FAVOURITE PICNIC AREA AMONGST SOLDIERS AND THEIR LADIES DURING GOVERNOR HUNTER'S REGIME. IT WAS REACHED BY PUNT AND, WHEN THEY WERE CARRIED ASHORE BY THEIR ESCORTS, EACH LADY HAD TO PAY A FORFEIT—ONE KISS.

THE BANKS
OF THE CONDAMINE

ANONYMOUS

Oh, hark the dogs are barking, love,
I can no longer stay,
The men are all gone mustering
And it is nearly day.
And I must be off by the morning light
Before the sun doth shine,
To meet the Sydney shearers
On the banks of the Condamine.

Oh Willie, dearest Willie,
I'll go along with you,
I'll cut off all my auburn fringe
And be a shearer, too,
I'll cook and count your tally, love,
While ringer-o you shine,
And I'll wash your greasy moleskins
On the banks of the Condamine.

Oh, Nancy, dearest Nancy,
With me you cannot go,
The squatters have given orders, love,
No woman should do so;
Your delicate constitution
Is not equal unto mine,
To stand the constant tigering
On the banks of the Condamine.

Oh, Willie, dearest Willie,
Then stay back home with me,
We'll take up a selection
And a farmer's wife I'll be:
I'll help you husk the corn, love,

And cook your meals so fine
You'll forget the ram-stag mutton
On the banks of the Condamine.

Oh, Nancy, dearest Nancy,
Please do not hold me back,
Down there the boys are waiting,
And I must be on the track;
So here's a good-bye kiss, love,
Back home here I'll incline
When we've shorn the last of the jumbucks
On the banks of the Condamine.

Excerpt from Memories of the Past: by a Lady in Australia, *written by Annie Baxter at Yesabba, Port Macquarie, New South Wales, c. 1842:*

. . . The servant woman whom I brought from Tasmania had been transported for life for forging a cheque on her uncle. She was very young and pretty. Our manservant had 'bought out' of the regiment at the same time we left, for the purpose of going with us to Port Macquarie. We had been there about three years when Supple, the man, came and asked leave to marry Mary; and my husband thought, as she was so much the younger of the two, it was a pity for her to throw herself away, so he spoke to her.

'Mary,' said he, 'what makes you think of marrying Supple, a man old enough to be your father—and such an ugly man, and you such a pretty girl?'

'Well, sir, John Supple is *not* a pretty man; but his manners! oh! sir, his manners!' said Mary.

We could say nothing to this, and manners carried the day.

It is quite well known that Ludwig Leichhardt's motivation for going to Australia was disappointment in love. In September 1840, he wrote in his diary that a certain Lucy Nicholson had become engaged to another man, adding:

So goes the one on whom all my hope of future domestic happiness depended. My heart runs over as I am forced to tear her image, roots and all, from my breast. She, whom I have during these three years cherished as man and wife, whom in the deepest recesses of my breast I have nourished with quiet warmth . . .

Leichhardt was not to be lucky in love in Australia, either. One of Australia's most tantalising might-have-been romances is hinted at in this letter from the dour explorer to Emmeline, youngest daughter of John Macarthur:

STROUD THE 12TH OCTOBER 1846
MY DEAR MISS MACARTHUR

I still fancy to hear the sounds of your silver ringing voice, and still believe to look into your smiling eye and the roguish friendship of Mr Forster [a neighbour] enabled me to learn by heart the outlines of your fair countenance. But since I received your kind letter and present I consider it my good right to cherish your memory and to brighten my lonely hours with recollections of you, my beautiful friend, whom I should wish to pray and to pray with your whole heart and soul for the welfare of Your most sincere friend.

LUDWIG LEICHHARDT

Young Emmie does not appear to have returned Leichhardt's feelings and, when he returned in 1848 and found her married, he curtailed his stay. Emmie noted, perhaps wistfully, that '. . . when he found me again as Mrs Leslie . . . I was the last woman to wish him God-speed . . . '

THE SITE OF COLLIT'S INN, AT THE FOOT OF MOUNT YORK ON OLD COX'S ROAD THROUGH THE BLUE MOUNTAINS, WAS THE BIRTHPLACE OF A POPULAR MUSICAL, 'COLLIT'S INN', IN THE LATE 1840S.

ACCORDING TO THE PLOT, AMELIA COLLIT LOVED A BUSHRANGER NAMED TOM. A MEDDLING CHAMBERMAID, ALSO ENAMOURED OF TOM, TOLD A HOT-TEMPERED YOUNG ENSIGN OF THE AFFAIR. THE FINAL SCENE, A DUEL BETWEEN THE TWO MEN, WAS A MASTERPIECE OF VICTORIAN MELODRAMA, WITH THE CHAMBERMAID BEING REJECTED BY THE ENSIGN, THE ENSIGN BEING REJECTED BY AMELIA AND TOM EXPIRING IN AMELIA'S ARMS. IN REAL LIFE AMELIA DID MARRY THE ENSIGN, AND THEIR GRAVESTONES MAY STILL BE FOUND IN THE TINY GRAVEYARD NEAR THE INN.

Though Welsh-born, Charles Harpur became one of Australia's foremost poets and was especially well known for the withering rhymed criticisms he directed at Australian senators. He was also very much in love with his wife, Mary, and their courtship and marriage provided material for much of his work. This rapturous sonnet was inspired by their 1841 wedding:

THE CONSUMMATION
CHARLES HARPUR

Mine after all—my Mary! Why should I
That most moved, sweet name any more disguise,
Now that beneath the conscious-seeming skies
My joy may spread itself as openly?
I weep—and fondly ask the reason why:
Thinking my happy heart in no such wise
Should keep effusing through my happy eyes,
Now that She's mine by an enduring tie!
Mine after all—my Mary! Lo, the Past
With all its doubt and dread and passionate sorrow
But travailed with Content! since thus at last
Love's whole light full into my lot is cast:
Even as the sun ariseth on the morrow
Out of the broken storm—cloudless and vast!

The marriage anticipated in David Blair's love letter to Annie Grant took place in 1852 and produced six children:

JUNE 17TH 1850
MY DEAREST ANNIE,

There are many things which I wish to say to you and which I *ought* to say to you, which nevertheless are better put upon paper than spoken directly. Grave long speeches are not the kind of intercourse that I like, any more than (I am sure) you would. Besides, it is not easy to be *very* sedate while sitting beside you, with your beautiful sunshiny countenance and most pleasant smile, and the delightful feeling of quiet happiness I have while talking to you. I am altogether too light-hearted when beside you, to put on a grave face and talk like—what I am—a philosopher. So I have been meditating about you (as usual) here in my attic for the last couple of hours and so I shove away the tiresome books, and begin the agreeable task of talking to you on paper.

That I do most truly and most entirely love you—as I never before loved a woman; as I never again can love a woman—I know you believe. However surprised you may have been at first, you fully believe this *now*. You have accepted all the love I had to bestow—valueless as I feel the gift to have been—and I *know* you have given me the priceless treasure of your true love in return. If we were less formal and less dilatory in settling this most delightful business than others are, at least we were fully as cordial and sincere as any others *could* be. Next to the happiness which I feel in possessing your affections, is the happiness springing from the feeling that you bestowed them upon me spontaneously and most willingly. I am perfectly satisfied and happy. The love of one such puresouled and affectionate girl as you are, was all I asked. I have found it, and I am content and more than content. You are satisfied with me, I know. You know me, short as our acquaintance has been, very thoroughly. You have seen all my character. There is nothing more to let you know, and nothing concealed from you. I am simply the book-loving, intellectual, earnest man, with fluent (sometimes eloquent) speech, and high thoughts, which you see me to be. I have no money, no friends, no 'prospects', no hopes of a 'situation under government'. But I have a strong belief that a man's life consists in quite other things than fine house, splendid dinner parties, carriage and all that. I carry this idea so far that I don't care much about these things—nor about the people who have them. I have a soul, and a Bible and a splendid sky above my head, and a magnificent vision forever floating before my mind of a glorious Heaven where all is light, and love, and joy . . .

Now, Annie Grant, what do you say to *that* portrait of an actual Lover, and possible Husband? Think over the whole affair, seriously. Look at both sides of the picture. And say whether you would choose to link your fortunes and your happiness with such a man, than take the probable chance of a Life Companion much handsomer, much younger, much richer and much more what the world calls 'respectable' . . . But, I beg a thousand pardons for the bare supposition. I do most entirely trust in your faithful love for me . . . I have drawn a picture of my 'inner man' which—upon looking it over again—is too flattering. I have faults—lots of faults. I know it well. But I do honestly say that I have no fault of a kind to mar the happiness of a lovely girl who trusts her all of earthly good to my keeping . . . I have *no* fault which would be the means of giving pain to a gentle and affectionate Wife. Where I loved, I should be trustful, tender and constant. I am sure I should be generous and tender even to the little failings—for we are all human—of the

One I loved. I never could be vindictive, nor irritable about trifles, nor morose or sullen, to Her. Oh no! I would aspire to make the pure passion by which I was bound in body and soul to Her, a worthy and exalted passion, as free as might be from all gross and sordid taint. I should try to live a noble and dignified life; happy myself, and making others happy, and thus tasting in all its exquisite sweetness

The joy of loving and being loved.

. . . There is one point which I am somewhat dubious about, after all. I don't think I ever told you—or you ever asked me—the important question which relates to my *age*. My conscience gives me a fillip about this. I *ought* to have told you: for *I* think *you* think I'm younger than I am. Don't be startled—still less shocked—least of all awfully frightened—if I tell you honestly that I have reason to believe I am—guess!—no, not 26, nor 27, nor 28, nor 29, but—actually 30!!! That's too bad, isn't it? But really I'm not to blame. In the first place, I can't help my age. In the second place, I thought—forgive this very ungallant avowal—I really *did* think you were more than 18¾. I thought—from your beautiful feminine grace—your thoroughly developed womanly beauty—that you were about 21. And I thought (thinks I) 'Well, only 9 years are not so frightful'; but eleven *is* too bad. However, I can only say . . . If you take me, you must just take me as I am . . . Well but you will say, if I am so old a soldier, why didn't I pitch my tent before now? There's the very point. Well you see, Annie Grant, I found it so difficult to carry the Ideal into everyday actual practice, that I had to wait until the Beau Ideal—the beautiful Realised Ideal—should come. To say truth . . . I have more than once had meaningful glances from bright eyes in the heads of pleasant countenanced young ladies cast upon me. Nay, I have even sat at tea, or at supper, or gone to picnic parties, with decidedly very loveable young ladies—who were so very condescending as to smile when I spoke to them, and to talk of my 'talents', and all that, and to wonder why I was so very self-absorbed, a bachelor, and so forth. But somehow there was sure to be something or other that whispered me that *here* I could not give my heart safely, and *there* it would not be altogether wise to plunge lip-deep in love . . . So I have escaped Scotfree from England. And here in Surry Hills, [Sydney NSW] I find the true living Ideal-Real at last. All that I ever dreamt of loveliness, and all I ever sighed for in pure affection, and innocent-heartedness, I find summed-up, concentrated, embodied, personified, realised, in the pleasant, attractive, agreeable, delightful, lovely, fascinating, bewitching, enchanting Annie Grant!! And so good night, my sweet love! I kiss you a thousand times. God for ever bless you!

Ever your faithful and devoted,
D. B.

Sophy Taylor's friends and relatives in England would have wondered about her life after she emigrated to Adelaide to marry Edward Cooke. She wrote this touching description of their meeting after a year's separation:

. . . I was prepared to meet a rough-looking creature almost from the bush at the Port [when I arrived], instead of which I was agreeably surprised when I found [Edward to be] a respectable colonial tradesman. He looked so nice, the only difference in his dress is a light cap with calico covering which almost everyone wears for coolness. Very few wear hats or anything else black, even umbrellas are covered with white calico to resist the heat . . .

I think he is more comical than ever. I was telling him the other day of someone in London who did not know that I was engaged to him, and he answered very dryly: 'I tell you Sophy, it was all very fine for you to tell the people that you were engaged, but I never engaged to have anyone half your size; you were a nice reasonable sized creature when I engaged to have you'! One day before we were married, I told him I knew when it came to the time I should go through the ceremony more courageously than he would. 'Well,' he said, 'if you look up in my face at the time very triumphantly as much as to say it's a case with you now Edward, I might feel disposed to cut away.' The fun we had before it was over! He used to make me laugh so much I could scarcely keep on walking.

I tell you these little things that you may know he is not much altered. I am very glad indeed that I came because we are, as I expected we would be, very happy together. I feel that it is also the right course. I did not think that he was quite so miserable because I did not come sooner, as people tell me he was. Sometimes when he has been invited to dine with a friend they tell me he would sit so thoughtful and scarcely speak. He tells me that when he received the last letter I sent, in which I asked him to come home as I must postpone my journey till another year, he never slept for *three nights*; but it's all over now and after so good a test we have all the more confidence in each other.

I don't suppose I shall ever forget meeting Edward at the ship. It happened that the day we arrived one of our passengers, Mr Willey, wishing to see the town of Adelaide, left his family and rode up from the Port; while here he came into the shop and bought some calico from Edward, little thinking who he was. Mr Willey happened to say he had arrived from England that morning. 'By what vessel?' asked Edward. '*Candahar*, sir,' said the stranger. At that Edward enquired if I was on board . . . Busy as he was he left the shop to the boy and came down to the Port that night, for he said he knew he should not sleep. When I heard his voice, just as it was getting dusk, asking for me in the 'tween decks, I rushed into my cabin for I was determined not to meet him in public, and when I put out my hand and asked him in he was almost breathless with excitement though he had ridden all the way. I could have fainted. After a little time he told me to put my bonnet on and away we strolled for a few hours by moonlight. After a hot supper we retired about 11 o'clock.

The moonlit nights here are delightful and I like the sort of life we lead. We do not have to study so much etiquette here, neither are we criticized for what we do. We can both do in fact just as we like. For instance, one warm evening before we were married, both being rather too tired to read after Edward had shut up the store, he laid his arm across my shoulder and away we strolled over the mountains at the back, he in his shirt-sleeves and I without a bonnet. We met not a creature to interrupt us, all was calm and still. I do enjoy such walks as these. Many we have had as pleasant, they always remind me of home.

HIS GIPPSLAND GIRL
WILL H. OGILVIE

Now, money was scarce and work was slack
And Love to his heart crept in,
And he rode away on the Northern track
To war with the World and win;
And he vowed by the locket upon his breast
And its treasure, one red-gold curl,
To work with a will in the farthest West
For the sake of his Gippsland girl.

The hot wind blows on the dusty plain
And the red sun burns above,
But he sees her face at his side again,
And he strikes each blow for Love:
He toils by the light of one far-off star,
For the winning of one white pearl,
And the swinging pick and the driving bar
Strike home for the Gippsland girl.

With aching wrist and a back that's bent,
With salt sweat blinding his eyes,
'Tis little he'd wreck if his life were spent
In winning so grand a prize;
And his shear-blades flash and over his hand
The folds of the white fleece curl,
And all day long he sticks to his stand
For the love of his Gippsland girl.

When the shearing's done and the sheds cut out
On Barwon and Narran and Bree;
When the shearer mates with the rouseabout
And the Union man with the free;
When the doors of the shanty, open wide,
An uproarious welcome hurl,
He passes by to the other side
For the sake of his Gippsland girl.

When summer lay brown on the Western land
He rode once more to the South,
Athirst for the touch of a lily hand
And the kiss of a rosebud mouth;
And he sang the songs that shorten the way,
And he envied not king or earl,
And he spared not the spur in his dappled grey
For the sake of his Gippsland girl.

At the garden gate when the shadows fell
His hopes in the dusk lay dead;
'Nellie? Oh! Surely you heard that Nell
Is married a month?' they said.
He spoke no word; with a dull, dumb pain
At his heart, and his brain awhirl,
He turned his grey to the North again
For the sake of his Gippsland girl.

And he rung the board in a Paroo shed
By the sweat of his aching brow,
And he blued his cheque, for he grimly said:
'There is nothing to live for now.'
And out and away where the big floods start
And the Darling dust-showers swirl,
There's a drunken shearer that broke his heart
Over a Gippsland girl.

As Long as Your Eyes are Blue

A. B. (Banjo) Paterson, 1891

Wilt thou love me, sweet, when my hair is grey,
And my cheeks shall have lost their hue?
When the charms of youth shall have passed away,
Will your love as of old prove true?
For the looks may change, and the heart may range,
And the love be no longer fond;
Wilt thou love with truth in the years of youth
And away to the years beyond?

O, I love you, sweet, for your locks of brown
And the blush on your cheek that lies—
But I love you most for the kindly heart
That I see in your sweet blue eyes—
For the eyes are signs of the soul within,
Of the heart that is leal and true,
And mine own sweetheart, I shall love you still,
Just as long as your eyes are blue.

For the locks may bleach, and the cheeks of peach
May be reft of their golden hue;
But mine own sweetheart, I shall love you still,
Just as long as your eyes are blue.

In My Home in Tasmania *(1853), Louisa Meredith gave detailed accounts of wooing amongst Australia's convict classes for the edification of those 'back home':*

As all my prisoner women-servants have had suitors in plenty, I have sometimes been amused by quietly observing the growing symptoms of the tender passion, as exemplified (in their class of life) by the unfailing presents and love-tokens offered by the enamoured swain as symbols of his sincere attachment, and signs of progress made . . . The presentation of a bonnet and ribbons I look upon as a decidedly serious advance, and in some cases a few yards of calico often give a grave aspect to the affair; a shawl, too, is considered a very affecting thing, and I have known a lace cap on the head exercise a mightly influence over the heart; but the grand conclusive stroke of all, the true love-philter, the unerring omen that bids me seek a new handmaiden—when the bolt of Cupid comes wrapped in flannel! Print gowns and new bonnets are, no doubt, shrewd pleaders; ribbons and lace, too, are insinuating things; and shawls and calico may mean much; but when the courtship takes the shape of flannel, I know the work of wooing has sped—the damsel's heart is won; and that the next thing will be John's awkward round-about request for leave to 'keep company with Mary'; which is very quickly followed by Mary's sheepish presentation of the 'memorial for marriage', with—'If you would please, ma'am, to ask the master to please to recommend us!' And married they are, shortly after, if the lover is in a situation to maintain a wife, which the superior powers very rightly desire to know before authorizing the marriage.

The Eureka Stockade incident, which occurred during Australia's goldrush days, saw a small band of poorly armed diggers clash with an overwhelming military force in their bid for justice and equality. On the eve of the battle the diggers' leader, Peter Lalor, sat down and wrote to the woman he loved, local schoolmistress Alicia Dunne:

Excerpt from *Southern Lights and Shadows:* being brief notes of three years' experience of social, literary and political life in Australia, by Frank Fowler (1859):

The great public resort of servantgalism in Sydney, is a place called 'Lover's Walk', situated in Hyde Park, and where from three to four hundred young ladies meet every Sunday night and carry on the most uproarious gambols with their male companions. This parade, on Sunday, is worse than our Hungerford Market used to be, and that was a disgrace to London. It is so thronged with lovers, ranging from ten to thirty years of age, that it is next to impossible for a quiet man, untroubled with the passion, to walk along. For rumpus and practical joke, it is like an Italian carnival, lacking the (substantial) sugar-plums. The girls are very fond of carrying lucifer matches and marking phosphorescent crosses and ghostly profiles on the backs of their dark-shawled rivals.

Ballarat November 30 1854
My Dear

Since my last, a most unfortunate state of things has arisen here. I mentioned that great excitement prevailed here, owing to the attempt of the magistrates to screen the murderer of a digger. That excitement has been still further increased by wicked licence hunting. The authorities have gone so far as to have had the diggers fired upon this morning, who, in self-defence, have taken up arms and are resolved to use them. In fact, my dear—to confess the truth, I am one amongst them. You must not be unhappy on this account. I would be unworthy of being called a man, I would be unworthy of myself, and above all I would be unworthy of you and your love, were I base enough to desert my companions in danger. Should I fall, I beseech you by your love for me—that love which has increased in proportion to my misfortunes—to shed but a single tear on the grave of one who has died in the cause of honour and liberty, and then forget me until we meet in heaven.

Farewell, and believe me, my dear
Yours until death,
Peter Lalor

After fleeing, wounded, from the stockade, Lalor went to Miss Dunne's house. He remained in hiding until the middle of the following year, when the pair married and bought a block of land in Ballarat.

The notorious bushranger Frank Gardiner had a long record of holding up
stagecoaches and horse stealing. He may have continued his career indefinitely had it
not been for an impassioned romance with Ben Hall's sister-in-law, Janet Brown.
According to Lancelot Booth in The Devil's Nightcap, Janet hid notes for Frank in
a hollow tree, including this fateful one before he robbed the Eugowra gold escort in
1862:

> . . . I am fully resolved, I am sick of this life of mine with a great old
> fool of a husband only in name. Whether you succeed in this your last
> venture or whether you fail, I am yours till death. If you should be shot,
> I shall follow you. But nothing will occur like that. Then away for a
> new life in a new land! Away with doubts and fears, and adieu to a
> hunted life my brave bushranger. The only suspense I shall suffer will be
> the lagging hours till I look into your bonny brown eyes. Adieu—no—
> au revoir . . .
>
> YOUR DEVOTED J.
> BURN THIS AT ONCE.

Gardiner was successful and the pair departed for Queensland with £20,000.
However, their whereabouts were discovered, largely because foolish Janet became
bored and could not resist boasting of her lover's exploits.

While much has been written of successful free colonists and emancipated men in Australia, little is known of the faceless, often illiterate convicts and the families they unwillingly left behind.

Dreary poverty forced Yorkshireman William Sykes to illegally poach game as food for his children. In 1865 he was arrested and shipped to Western Australia, never to see his wife, Myra, again. Her wistful letters touch the heart with their longing and despair, including this first, written while William was awaiting transportation to Fremantle:

MASBRO' 19 MARCH 1867
MY DEAR HUSBAND—

I have this afternoon received your letter and am glad to hear from you—I heard yesterday that there was a letter from you at Park-gate and wrote off immediately to the Governor of the Portsmouth prison asking him to kindly send me word if he would what was the latest day I could see you . . . I hope the governor will either send me a reply or allow you to do so, for I will leave no means untried to get to see you if there is time but if I was at the expense only to be too late when I got there it will be a serious loss to me situated as I am . . .

Although we are separated there is no one I value and regard equal to You—and I should like you to still have the same feeling towards me, and if there is ever a chance of our being permitted to join you again even though it be in a far off land, both the children and myself will most gladly do so—Mr Bone has written to his wife to get the childrens likenesses taken for him, to take away with him I should like to have ours if you are allowed the same privilige—Will you let me know? I cannot give you up. I live in the hope of our being together again somewhere before we end our days—My best love to you, the children also send their love to you, and love and remembrance from all friends your affectionate wife—Myra Sykes

William Strutt 1825–1915, *Gold Diggers Receiving a Letter From Home*, c.1860

Sadly, Myra was unable to make her final farewells at Portsmouth, probably due to the time involved in travelling there. Although the couple never met again, correspondence continued and Myra's faithful love never wavered, as evidenced by this excerpt from one of her letters written shortly before William's death nearly thirty years later:

> . . . and my Dear Husban I sends my nearest and Dearest Love to you and all the children with A 1000 Loves and kiss wish we may meet again ho that We cold in this World . . .

A broken love affair with a girl named Rose Bennett filled poet Henry Kendall with gloom. Like many jilted lovers before and since, he wrote poetry to assuage his feelings.

AT NIGHTFALL (1870)

Ah Love! There is no passion like the first:
I feel it when I breathe your slow sweet name,
I know it when I hear the songs you loved,
It burns me when I pass you in the street;
In all my dreams your shadow floats about,
In all my walks your presence fills the time,
In all my verse there is a trace of you;
And since our alienation I have felt
That sense of loss which never leaves a man,
But kills his pleasure in the glad green earth.

FROM ROSE LORRAINE (1870)

. . . I keep a faded ribbon string
You used to wear about your throat;
And of this pale, this perished thing
I think I know the threads by rote.
God help such love! To touch your hand,
To loiter where your feet might fall,
You marvellous girl, my soul would stand
The worst of hell—its fires and all . . .

Eccentric E. W. Cole held accepted customs in contempt and had little use for staid Melbourne society. The establishment was, therefore, duly shocked when the irascible fellow decided to acquire a wife via a full column advertisement in the Melbourne Herald *on July 3 1875:*

A GOOD WIFE WANTED
TWENTY POUNDS REWARD
POSITIVELY BONA FIDE
I, EDWARD WILLIAM COLE
OF THE
BOOK ARCADE BOURKE-STREET
WISH TO OBTAIN A PERSON FOR A WIFE
WITH THE FOLLOWING CHARACTERISTICS:

SHE MUST BE A SPINSTER of thirty-five or six years of age, good tempered, intelligent, honest, truthful, sober, chaste, cleanly, neat, but not extravagantly or absurdly dressy; industrious, frugal, moderately educated and a lover of home. Any respectable, well-intentioned person who from the range of their observation can conscientiously recommend to me an unengaged woman answering the above description will, in the event of such a marriage taking place between us in consequence of such information, receive my sincere thanks and the above reward directly such marriage takes place. This may be thought by many an absurd, perhaps unusual, way of looking for a wife; and I am quite sensible that I may be laughed at, but the thoughtful will not laugh, the most they will do in that direction will be to smile good-humouredly for they know that whilst the best thing a man can have is a good wife, and the worst thing a bad wife, yet, in most cases, a very irrational principle of selection is followed, for that nineteen out of twenty of the unions that take place originate from the merest accidents of life, from a chance meeting at a ball, at a relation's, at a friend's, at a neighbor's, etc. I take that I believe to be the most reasonable course, of looking around to find and when found, of ascertaining by inquiry, the exact character a woman bears in her neighborhood, and amongst those who know her, before I enter into dissoluble intimacy with her; and I have no hesitation in advertising for, critically examining into the character of one who is to be my partner for life, than I should have were I merely advertising for a business partner: and, if, by advertising, I get a good, suitable wife instead of any unsuitable one, which I should very likely get in the usual way, my temporary exposure is well indemnified and my twenty pounds well spent . . .

Please address any communication to

E. W. COLE
BOOK ARCADE
BOURKE STREET

Three days later, he had his reply; the lady, Miss Eliza Frances Jordan, wrote:

Sir, I have very carefully read your letter in the *Herald* and I think it is a sensible one. I want someone to love and take care of me, someone I can look up to and respect . . . I have made the acquaintance of a few gentlemen in Victoria and what I have met do not come up to my ideas of a good husband. I do not care so much about a pretty face (though I like to see one as well as most people). I would sooner have good sense and good temper any day. I am not pretty myself, for I am a little dark thing with dark eyes and hair, and nearly 30 years old.

I have received a very good education, and have been brought up to do everything from making a pudding to playing the piano. I am rather hard to please, for I intend to look before I leap. You could not blame me for that . . .

Irene Brown 1898–1984, *Portrait of a Woman Writing*, 1940

E. W. Cole proposed to Eliza upon meeting her; they married shortly afterwards and had six children.

A Tell-tale Tryst

Will H. Ogilvie

O who was it saddled White Star last night,
And who was it saddled White Star?
You can read his track to the rails and back
And down the creek ever so far.
O, moonlight is lover's light, Somebody knows,
And witch-time the season to woo,
And down in the bends where the kurrajong grows
The tracks have been trodden by two!

O, who was it galloped White Star last night,
When gold stars jewelled the sky?
You can see the brand of saddle and band
In sweat that is clotted and dry.
O, Somebody raced, with the world asleep,
To a tryst that Somebody knew,
And over the blue-grass fetlock-deep
The white hoofs scattered the dew!

O, who was it fastened White Star last night
To a bough of the kurrajong tree?
The deep-set grooves of his restless hooves
Are there for the world to see.
O, Somebody left him for true love's sake,
And Somebody left him long,
For horses may hunger and bridles break
When true love fashions her song!

O, who was it fondled White Star last night
When Somebody whispered adieu,
And plaited the grey of his mane in a way
That never those grey locks grew?
And who was it bent from his saddle-bow
To the plea of an upturned face,
While down in the bend where the kurrajongs grow
The world stood still for a space?

O, the lover who saddled White Star last night
It is very easy to guess,
For his face is bright with a new-found light
And a joy that his eyes confess.
O, Somebody met in the moonlight snow
Someone that cared to be kissed,
And the veriest dolt in the world may know
Who rode to the moonlight tryst!

Harold Cazneaux 1878–1953, *The Veil, Blue Mountains*

THE DROVER'S SWEETHEART

HENRY LAWSON (1891)

An hour before the sun goes down
Behind the ragged boughs,
I go across the little run
And bring the dusty cows;
And once I used to sit and rest
Beneath the fading dome,
For there was one that I loved best
Who'd bring the cattle home.

Our yard is fixed with double bails;
Round one the grass is green,
The Bush is growing through the rails,
The spike is rusted in;
It was from there his freckled face
Would turn and smile at me;
For he'd milk seven in the race
While I was milking three.

He kissed me twice and once again
And rode across the hill,
The pint-pots and the hobble-chain
I hear them jingling still . . .
About the hut the sunlight fails,
The fire shines through the cracks—
I climb the broken stockyard rails
And watch the bridle-tracks.

And he is coming back again—
He wrote from Evatt's Rock;
A flood was in the Darling then
And foot-rot in the flock.
The sheep were falling thick and fast

A hundred miles from town,
And when he reached the line at last
He trucked the remnant down.

And so he'll have to stand the cost;
His luck was always bad,
Instead of making more, he lost
The money that he had;
And how he'll manage, Heaven knows
(My eyes are getting dim)
He says—he says—he don't—suppose
I'll want—to—marry—him.

As if I wouldn't take his hand
Without a golden glove—
Oh! Jack, you men won't understand
How much a girl can love.
I long to see his face once more—
Jack's dog! Thank God, it's Jack!—
(I never thought I'd faint before)
He's coming—up—the track.

Frederick McCubbin 1855–1917, *Home Again*, 1884

THE LOVE LETTER (AUSTRALIAN ETIQUETTE, 1885)

Of this it may only be said, that while it may be expressive of sincere esteem and affection, it should be of a dignified tone, and written in such style, that if it should ever come under the eyes of others than the party to whom it was written, there may be found in it nothing of which the writer may be ashamed, either of silliness or of extravagant expression.

BASHFUL GLEESON
EDWARD DYSON

From her home beyond the river in the parting of the hills,
Where the wattle's fleecy blossom surged and scattered in the breeze,
And the tender creepers twined about the chimneys and the sills,
And the garden flamed with colour like an Eden through the trees,
She would come along the gully, where the ferns grew golden fair,
In the stillness of the morning, like the spirit of the place,
With the sun-shafts caught and woven in the meshes of her hair,
And the pink and white of heathbloom sweetly blended in her face.

She was fair, and small, and slender-limbed, and buoyant as a bird,
Fresh as wild, white, dew-dipped violets where the bluegums shadow goes,
And no music like her laughter in the joyous bush was heard,
And the glory of her smile was as sunbeam in a rose.

Ben felt mighty at the windlass when she watched him hauling stuff,
And she asked him many questions, 'What was that?' and 'Why was this?'
Though his bashfulness was painful, and he answered like a muff,
With his foolish 'My word, Missie!' and his 'Beg your pardon, Miss.'

He stood six foot in his bluchers, stout of heart and strong of limb;
For her sake he would have tackled any man or any brute;
Of her half a score of suitors none could hold a light to him,
And he owned the richest hole along the Bullock lead to boot.

Yet while Charley Mack and Hogan, and the Teddywaddy skite
Put in many pleasant evenings at 'The Bower', Ben declined,
And remained a mere outsider, and would spend on half the night,
Waiting, hid behind the trees, to watch her shadow on the blind.

He was laughed at on the river and as far as Kiley's Still
They would tell of Bashful Gleeson who was 'gone on' Kitty Dwyer,
But, beyond defeating Hogan in a pleasant Sunday mill,
Gleeson's courtship went no further till the morning of the fire.

MEETING
THE MAILMAN.
397. Kerry. Sydney.

We were called up in the darkness, heard a few excited words;
In the garden down the flat a Chow was thumping on a gong;
There were shouts and cooeys on the hills and cries of startled birds,
But we saw the gum leaves redden and that told us what was wrong.

O'er 'The Bower' the red cloud lifted as we sprinted for the punt
Gleeson took the river for it in the scanty clothes he wore.
Dwyer was madly calling for Kitty when we joined the men in front;
Whilst they questioned, hoped and wondered, Ben was smashing at the door.

He went in amongst the smoke, and found her room, but some have said
That he dared not pass the threshold—that he lingered in distress,
Game to face the fire, but not to pluck sweet Kitty from her bed
And he knocked again and asked her timidly to 'please get up and dress.'

Once again he called, and waited till a keen flame licked his face;
Then a Spartan-like devotion welled within the simple man,
And he shut his eyes and ventured to invade the sacred place,
Found the downy couch of Kitty, clutched an armful up, and ran.

True or not, we watched and waited and our hearts grew cold and sick
Ere he came, we barely caught him as the flame leapt in his hair.
He had saved the sheets, a bolster, and the blankets and the tick;
But we looked in vain for Kitty—pretty Kitty wasn't there!

And no wonder: whilst we drenched him as he lay upon the ground,
And her mother wailed entreaties that it wrung our hearts to hear,
Hill came panting with the tidings that Miss Kitty had been found,
Clad in white and quite unconscious, 'mid the saplings at the rear.

We're not certain how it happened, but I've heard the women say
That 'twas Kitty's work. She saw him when the doctor's left, they vow,
Swathed in bandages and helpless, and she kissed him where he lay.
Anyhow, they're three years married, and he isn't bashful now.

Alexander Crawford emigrated to Australia from Belfast in 1880. In Ballarat he met his cousin, Lillie Matthews, and they fell in love. Well aware of the family's opposition to cousins marrying, they kept their feelings quiet while Alexander established himself on a station in Western Australia. Much tender correspondence ensued, including the following:

13 APRIL 1882
MY DARLING LILLIE

. . . I do hope I will be successful in this station. The last manager lost nearly £500 a year on it but everyone says it was through bad management. When I come to think of it, it seems a risky undertaking for one with so little experience as myself to undertake to manage and bring a station, in a state of utter disorder, into good order. I have scarcely had one year's experience but if close attention to it and hard work will do anything towards making it pay it shall not be lacking on my part. And I am the more encouraged when I think it is not myself alone I am working for but for the *dearest girl living*. Oh, Lillie, *my own true love*, I would undergo anything for your sweet sake and count it but pleasure if I but brought you the nearer to me. I often think what would life be to me now without the *love of my Lillie*. I managed to get along in a kind of way before but now it would be misery indeed. Tis the sweetest thought I have that before long I hope to take you to myself for better, there will be no worse in it. Sure there won't. Do tell me more about yourself in your letters. Fill them up about Lillie, commence with Lillie, end with Lillie and fill the space between with the same subject, and you may add a postscript about her, too, and it will not be too much. It is a subject I never weary reading about, writing about, or speaking about, so satisfy me in this respect my little girl . . . I do wish I could make my mustache grow longer. It sticks at the one length, much to my disgust. Is not this vanity worse than a girl, I fancy I can hear you say. Perhaps by the time you see me next it may have stretched a little and you may not be able to get at my lips. How will that do! . . .

After five long years of waiting, the pair were married in Victoria in 1885. Alexander was later to confide in his brother that:

I am almost four years married now and I think I can truly say that Lillie has never cost me one minute, one second of unhappiness . . . you cannot know the happiness that is to be enjoyed in knowing there is one being dependent upon you who loves you more than all the world beside and whose interest is yours and yours is hers. I wish I had married five years sooner.

Sadly, Lillie died only two years later.

This poem accompanied the letter Herbert Curlewis sent his wife-to-be, Ethel Turner, author of Seven Little Australians, *on Christmas Day 1891.*

DEC 1891

Dear lady mine, the coming years
To me but happiness can bring
For with your love no evil thing
May come to me till life nears
The quiet of its long evening.

But, sweet, will you still be content?
I dare not think it will be so.
When my unworthiness you know
Have you no fear you may repent
The promise made then long ago?

And yet, My Ethel, it may be
That by your love more noble made,
I shall not vainly love essayed
To keep God's Sacred gift to me,
Perchance no need to feel afraid.

Yes God, whose sweetest saint you are,
Will keep you safe whate'er befall
And would his gift to me recall
If there were danger I should mar
The life He cares for most of all.

All useless, sweet—there is no way
To speak the thoughts that overflow
Thoughts I shall never make you know,
And this alone I find to say
Sweetheart, I love, I love you so.

H . R . C .

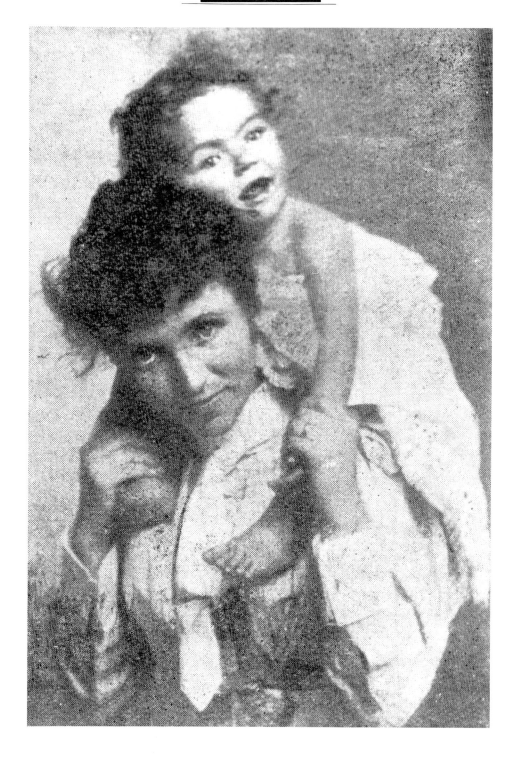

TO YOU
MARY GILMORE

Walking down the roadway
Me along o' you,
My hand in your hand,
Like we used to do;

Moonlight or sunlight,
Step and step, us two;
Harp-strings wasn't in it!
Living, through and through.

Little touchings closer,
Knocks, and bumps and starts,
All the hot blood racing
Through our eager hearts.

Hands so warm together,
Tongues half shy of talk:
Didn't seem to matter
When we used to walk.

Now I'd give the world and
everything afloat,
Just for the road again,
And the breath of your coat!

YOU A-WANTIN' ME

MARY GILMORE

You a-wantin' me,
Me a-wantin' you!
What's we waitin' for?
Life is wearin' through.

What's we waitin' for?
Lookin' still and sad?
Life ain't watchin' round,
Hopin' we'll be glad.

Time's no good to us,
Life ain't nothin' sweet,
Me a-mopin' here,
You across the street!

What should come between,
Partin' of us two—
You a-wantin' me,
Me a-wantin' you?

Kiss me on the mouth,
Kiss me, lovin'-fair;
What's we waitin' for
No one else will care!

What's we waitin' for?
Kiss me straight and true;
You a-wantin' me,
Me a-wantin' you!

Born Mary Cameron near Goulburn in 1865, Mary Gilmore travelled to the 'New Australia' settlement in Paraguay which aimed to be a model socialist community. While there she wrote most affectionately to Henry Lawson:

LA COLONIE 'COSME'
PARAGUAY, SOUTH AMERICA
VIA NZ AND MONTE VIDEO
5 AUGUST 1896

DEAR HARRY

I've got such a lot to say to you that I write on a postcard in order to say something. I am glad about your book but I haven't seen anything approaching a criticism of it, no one having sent me any papers. As for you, I believe you forgot me—but I know you didn't—only you might have sent me a copy of the book. Send me one anyway. How is it going? . . . I'd give a lot to see you here. The place teems with copy, the life makes it. I wish to Heaven I could write it up, I could cry when I see how it goes to waste. We are all original, everyone of us but as life becomes easier it will grow more commonplace and none but a see-er [sic] can write of us as we are now.

Communism as we have it is alright, Harry, and we are getting on—slowly, of course, but in a year or two what now is will have gone, drowned by prosperity. And the country—it is a constant wonder to me, so beautiful, so rich in bird [life] and plants. And the history!—and the stories of the war. If you were only here, Henry. Don't let someone else snap your chances. Come while the field is new—as a visitor, I mean, though I'd like you to come for good only I don't think you would. I am satisfied with life anyway and wish everyone found life as good as I do. Come if you can, dear old friend. You know I wouldn't ask you if I didn't think it was worth it—even from your standpoint.

M.J. CAMERON
P.S. I DIDN'T GET MARRIED.

Despite the intriguing tone of the letter—and the cryptic postscript—Mary married a Victorian shearer named William Gilmore six months later. The marriage did not last and her husband and only son departed for Queensland as Mary pursued her literary career. Perhaps Harry had something of this in mind when he penned 'The Sliprails and the Spur'.

THE SLIPRAILS
AND THE SPUR
HENRY LAWSON (1899)

The colours of the setting sun
Withdrew across the Western land—
He raised the sliprails, one by one,
And shot them home with trembling hand;
Her brown hands clung—her face grew pale—
Ah! Quivering chin and eyes that brim!
One quick, fierce kiss across the race,
And 'Goodbye, Mary!' 'Goodbye, Jim!'

On he rides hard to race the pain
Who rides from love, who rides from home;
But he rides slowly home again,
Whose heart has learnt to love and roam.

And hand upon the horse's mane,
And one foot in the stirrup set,
And, stooping back to kiss again,
With 'Goodbye, Mary! Don't you fret!
When I come back'—he laughed for her—
'We do not know how soon 'twill be;
I'll whistle as I round the spur—
You let the sliprails down for me.'

She gasped for sudden loss of hope,
As, with a backward wave to her,
He cantered down the grassy slope
And swiftly round the dark'ning spur.
Black-pencilled panels standing high,
And darkness fading into stars,
And, blurring fast against the sky,
A faint white form beside the bars.

And often at the set of sun,
In winter bleak and summer brown,
She'd steal across the little run,
And shyly let the sliprails down.
And listen there when darkness shut
The nearer spur in silence deep;
And when they called her from the hut
Steal home and cry herself to sleep.

And he rides hard to dull the pain
Who rides from one who loves him best . . .
And he rides slowly back again,
Whose restless heart must rove for rest.

Feisty parliamentarian Patrick McMahon Glynn was renowned in the House for his oratory skills, a heritage of his Irish forebears. He put this 'gift of the gab' to good use when wooing Miss Abigail Dynon:

7 DECEMBER 1897

DEAR MISS DYNON

I suppose it would do poor justice to the reputation my countrymen bear for courage—though in this case it may be called audacity—if I did not risk, as so many others in other cases have, with better or worse fortune done, the inevitable question. The world is made up of incompatibles, or rather contradictions; without the Union of opposites there would be no possibility of the average that makes progress. I am, in most of the qualities that build a character, at one pole, you at the other; but your sex is born to redeem, and Goodness Knows there is a big field for redemption in my case. Well, you can well think that I am, for once at all events in my life, in a bit of a muddle. I have written pamphlets, leading articles, essays, etc., by the mile, but never before put in writing the impertinence of a proposal of marriage. And this has to be done, at the table of the Legislative Assembly of New South

Wales, with the Federal Convention sitting, and Mr Lyne, within a yard of me, pouring on the too-thinly protected top of my head, a niagra [sic] of figures. However, I must attempt it.

Well Dear Miss Dynon, to be candid, which indeed is my dearest desire. I heard of you six or seven years ago, and from what a lady who knew you well said of you then, I know, if on meeting you I did not feel it instinctively, that you are as deserving of the reputation you bear as I am under the estimate . . . You unfortunately—or, rather perhaps, fortunately for myself—know little of me; that is, outside my reputation as a public man. But as far as I can say it, I feel I am a Bohemian in temperament, fond of the softer—I don't like to say poetic—side of life; liable, like many of my too romantic countrymen to extremes of spirit, by no means correct as the world goes, but at all events capable of discerning if not following, the Right. The girl that takes me will deserve an indulgence—a dispensation from purgatory, so that I may have at least a negative recommendation . . .

But I find, with my usual lack of pluck in matters outside my line, I am becoming all preface. The Sum of it all is this, if you consent to marry me, Miss Dynon, you will, for the sacrifice, deserve Heaven, and probably save me from somewhere else. May I ask you to do so. I am by no means well off—but why should I say that to you—but I can and do work, and though, if I may use the term for the Sake of its great expressiveness, devil-may-care in most matters, will try under the great responsibility, to become financially orthodox, I don't care the proverbial rap for the Ceremonial side of life.

If you consent to be my wife—a great word—why should we not be married at once. It will have the advantage for me that the matter will be inevitably settled before you know too much of me . . . If you have me, I can honestly promise you to give you no divided heart and to live no double life. You will know me, for good or bad, as I am.

Well, if you bless me, I will with your consent, go for you on Friday, marry on Saturday and return same day. If you will come—anyhow I wish you would—over at once, so much the better. We can be married on the arrival of the train. My friend Mr O'Malley will give me away; I hope he has not done so already. This is a lot to ask, but the occasion is my great excuse. I am not my own master now—we are the Servants of the Nation and its destinies. Besides, as I said, I know you thoroughly— and after we can call each other wife and husband; well, what does the unorthodox way of settling the bond matter.

In Hopes of a reply that will enable me to really begin to live, I am Dear Miss Dynon,

Your admirer and friend under any circumstances,

P. McM. GLYNN

'Dear Miss Dynon' did indeed accept Glynn's proposal, and the jubilant bridegroom advised his mother belatedly of the proceedings:

13 SEPTEMBER 1897

MY DEAR MOTHER

We are again in the thick of the Federal Convention work, the second or Sydney sitting being now on. It is to consider the amendments suggested by the various Australian Parliaments to the Bill drafted by the First, the Adelaide Convention. I accomplished rather a record last week. On Tuesday, during the Sitting, I wrote a proposal of marriage to a girl whom I had only spoken to once; had a telegram accepting on Wednesday; made what the audience considered a great speech on Thursday at 5.30pm; took the 7.15pm Express to Melbourne same night, got married on Saturday and returned same day, arriving here on Sunday. You will think I am mad. Perhaps a little. She is at all Events what will please you; a Catholic, a good one, with enough religion for the two of us. She has been round Europe several times and spoke French to the Pope for half an hour. I believe she is well off but I'm hanged if I know and didn't care. I hope I won't pull her down from Heaven.

But the Bell rings the House together again, so I must, with love, say Goodbye.

YOUR AFFECTIONATE SON
P. McM. GLYNN

AND SHE WAKES FROM HER DREAM.

AH, THE WAKING IS SAD,

FOR THE TEARS THAT IT BRINGS,

AND SHE KNOWS 'TIS HER DEAD BABY'S SPIRIT THAT SINGS:

"COME, MAMMA! COME!

QUICK! FOLLOW ME!

STEP OUT ON THE LEAVES OF THE WATER—LILY!"

HENRY LAWSON
November 1890

I Am Shut Out
of Mine Own Heart

CHRISTOPHER BRENNAN (1897)

I am shut out of mine own heart
because my love is far from me,
nor in the wonders have I part
that fill its hidden empery:

the wildwood of adventurous thought
and lands of dawn my dream had won,
the riches out of Faery brought
are buried with our bridal sun.

And I am in a narrow place,
and all its little streets are cold,
because the absence of her face
has robb'd the sullen air of gold.

My home is in a broader day:
at times I catch it glistening
thro' the dull gate, a flower'd play
and odour of undying spring:

the long days that I lived alone,
sweet madness of the springs I miss'd,
are shed beyond, and thro' them blown
clear laughter, and my lips are kiss'd:

—and here, from mine own joy apart,
I wait the turning of the key:—
I am shut out of mine own heart
because my love is far from me.

David Davies 1864–1939, *From A Distant Land*, 1889

Steele Rudd's tales, which first appeared in On Our Selection *in 1899, pithily expressed the spirit of early Australia:*

SARAH'S COURTSHIP

Steele Rudd

When Dad kicked Billy Bearup out of our door and broke up a dance with him and some days later chased him through the sliprails at the point of a loaded gun, Billy didn't come back to see Sarah any more— at least not while Dad was about. But whenever Dad was away somewhere, Billy would turn up in clean clothes and a broad smile. How Billy could tell when Dad was to be absent from home we never could understand, it was a mystery to us.

'Intuition,' Joe suggested one day, when we were discussing Billy and Sarah at the plough.

But Tom suspected Sarah herself. 'She lets him know,' he said.

Bill discredited Tom's theory. 'No,' Bill said, 'I've been there when he's come along and she's alluz been more surprised to see him than anyone else.'

'Bosh!' Joe sniggered. 'She surprised!'

Joe was an authority on girls and their funny little ways. Joe courted a girl once himself—courted her hard and earnestly for two years—courted her until she accepted a ring and a side-saddle from him—and got married to another fellow.

Time went by and Sarah became discontented. She grew bad-tempered, too, and made the place miserable. She complained bitterly to Mother one evening of Dad's inhospitable attitude towards Billy, said she couldn't see why Billy shouldn't be allowed to come into the house like anyone else, and shed a lot of big tears over him.

'And he's going to come,' she blubbered desperately, 'and if father dares to say another word to him or does anything against him I'll go away—I'll leave home—I won't stay in this place—I won't put up with it, I won't, I won't.'

'Nonsense, child,' Mother said kindly, 'don't be a foolish girl. I'll speak to your father about it, and I'm sure he won't mind.'

And Mother was always as good as her word. She went straight away and spoke to Dad.

Dad was sitting on the veranda reading the paper when Mother started to speak to him. Before she had finished he was standing on tiptoes glaring at her like an infuriated old-man kangaroo.

'Never!' he roared. 'Never! To the devil with him!'

Mother came away from him and sought Sarah again.

'Leave it be for a while,' she whispered nervously, 'and I'll see him tomorrow.'

Sarah left it for a while—left it for months. Mother left it altogether.

Dad went to town one morning, intending to stay there a couple of days. He was barely out of sight when Billy Bearup rode up to the house and sat on his horse talking to Sarah. Sarah was pleased to see Billy and asked him wasn't he going to get off . . .

'Got to go all the way down to Peterson's Pocket yet,' he added, 'looking for a couple of steers we lost.' Then Billy looked down along the road that Dad had taken and, satisfied that Dad was well out of sight, dismounted and fastened his horse to the front palings and followed Sarah inside. After a while the sun and the lost steers went out of Billy's mind and he waited for dinner. He waited till the afternoon. He lounged about the house, sometimes talking to Mother, but more often to Sarah. At intervals Mother would look out of the door and, noticing the unfortunate horse standing in the broiling sun, stamping holes in the earth with his hoofs and flick-flicking at the flies with his bit of a tail, would invite Billy to put the animal in the stable and give him a feed, and Billy would drawl, 'Oh, he's orright, Mrs Rudd, I'll be goin' in a minute, anyway.'

About three o'clock Mother left Bill and Sarah together in the dining-room, and said she'd go and do some ironing. Mother had no ironing to do; it had all been done the day before. But Mother was always considerate where young people were concerned. Mother had been young herself once. And Billy and Sarah when Mother departed were sitting far apart. Several chairs and a corner of the table divided them. But distance didn't lend any enchantment to Billy's view of Sarah. It only made him uncomfortable. It made Sarah uncomfortable, too.

'Them's big geraniums,' Billy said, drawing Sarah's attention to some withered flowers that had been standing in a vase on the table for nearly a week. Any other time Billy wouldn't have wasted words on the finest flowers that ever grew.

'Aren't they pretty?' Sarah answered, jumping out of her chair and leaning on the table, and tenderly fingering the drooping geraniums as though she really admired them. Billy left his chair and leant on the table, too, fingering the geraniums. He also fingered Sarah's hair caressingly. And when Sarah didn't mind, Billy stole his arm quietly round her waist and squeezed her, and made her sigh, and his cheek rested against hers, and he was murmuring things to her when a heavy footstep was heard ascending the front veranda steps. And a voice called 'Hullo, Rowdy', in greeting to the dog. Billy and Sarah suddenly separated.

'Heavens!' Sarah gasped, jumping round and shoving Billy from her.

Pen couldn't describe the look that came into Billy's face.

'How can I get out?' he gasped, dancing round the table.

There were only two ways for Billy to get out, one through the door leading into Mother's bedroom, the other through the door leading into Dad's open arms.

'Under the table—quick,' Sarah said, seeing Billy hesitate.

But Billy had no courage or presence of mind when in a tight place; he had no courage or presence of mind when in any kind of place. He darted at the door leading to Mother's bedroom, threw it open, and rushed recklessly in. Mother was in the room. She was changing her clothes. She got a great start, and screamed. Billy got a great start, too, when he saw Mother, and rushed out again.

'The table—the table,' Sarah gasped again.

But Billy was deaf and blind and furious. His wild staring eyes rested on the open door and on the form of Dad pausing on the mat to pat the dog. He bounded for the door. Dad at the same time turned from the dog, and his burly form blocked the way. Billy didn't hesitate.

'*Whaht?*' roared Dad, recognising Billy as the latter bore down upon him. '*You* here?'

Then there was a great thud. Billy went for Dad, low, dived between his legs, and knocked him out onto the veranda. Dad got a great surprise, and yelled and clutched for Billy, but Billy slipped through Dad's arms and bounded down the steps and, mounting the horse, galloped away. Dad got up off his back and bellowed and, throwing bad language about, rushed inside to procure the gun. But before he could drag the weapon from its place on the wall Billy had disappeared over the horizon.

'I'll shoot him yet—the damn scoundrel!' Dad raved, putting the weapon away again. 'I'll shoot him like a wallaby.'

And Sarah in her room, hiding behind the curtains of her bed, trembled like a leaf, and broke out into large lumps of perspiration.

Three months passed away . . .

Dad, walking under the clothes-line one day after Sarah had hung out the washing, picked up a piece of notepaper with writing and perfume on it. Dad turned the paper over and over and looked at the address and signature, then frowned fiercely on it. 'The devil!' he muttered, and went onto the veranda and, sitting in an easy chair, began to spell through the curious document.

My dearest, sweatest Sara (it said) *it's foar nites sins we see each uther, and I'm longen to see you once moare. Meet me after supper too nite deer at the wite gait. Doant forget; doent dissuppoin me. When do the old chap go off some plaise agen.*

'Aha,' Dad broke out, growing interested, 'Aha!' Then he continued to spell:

I ope the old bare stays away altogether nex time (Dad grew very red in the face) *Give the ole dog me luv.*

'Damn his insolence,' Dad snorted.

An' take the saime yerself, and doant forget to be at the gait to meet your trooest Billy. 'Ow did yer like me foto I sent you.

'The damn scoundrel,' Dad said savagely, 'I'll meet him—I'll meet him.'

Then, muttering murderous threats, Dad made his way to the clothes-line again, and threw Sarah's love letter down where he had found it, and went away swearing to himself. He had scarcely left the spot when Sarah, bare-headed, and rummaging in her dress pockets, came running out with an anxious look on her face. You would think she had just received word that some bank in which she had a million of money deposited had failed. With her eyes fixed on the ground, she tracked herself to the barn and back, then to the woodheap, and to the water-tank, and back to the barn again.

Dad scowled, and watched Sarah out of the corner of his eye. Sarah crossed the yard several times.

'What's the matter with y'?' Dad growled at her.

'Dropped an old brooch somewhere, that's all,' Sarah murmured, colouring to her ears.

'I thought maybe it were y' head,' and Dad turned away. But he looked round again just in time to see Sarah pounce on the paper, and stuff it hurriedly into her bosom.

Sarah had supper ready early for us that night, and displayed a lot of anxiety to get the meal over.

'Hurry up and let me get cleared away,' she said, when Bill and Tom hung over their tea arguing about horses. 'I've got a lot of work to do tonight—and you haven't anything.'

Dad looked hard at Sarah and said nothing. And when everyone had finished Sarah rushed the things away to the kitchen and, starting to sing and whistle alternately, waded into the washing-up.

After supper Dad walked up and down the veranda for a long while, thinking hard. Then he called Barty, and told him to go and find the greenhide whip.

'What do you want it for, Dad?' Barty asked, arriving with a short, heavy 'slogger', belonging to Joe.

'Never mind, never mind, leave it there.' And Dad walked up and down some more.

Barty threw the whip on the chair and went off wondering. Then

Dad stepped quietly off the veranda, and, armed with the greenhide 'slogger', sauntered down towards the white gate.

There was a cold easterly wind blowing. The moon came up over the Great Dividing Range like a huge ball of fire, and the dogs barked and howled dismally at it. Possums squeaked in the box-trees that fringed the corn paddock, and flying-foxes on noiseless wings circled round and round the garden. The big white gate creaked on its hinges and opened wide and someone came though it, leading a horse. Dad paused for a moment to listen, then, grasping the greenhide firmly, hurried forward. The horse's rump was turned towards Dad; the person leading the animal turned to fasten the gate. At Dad's approach, the horse twisted nervously about and pulled on the reins. The man left the gate, and held firmly to the bridle.

'You—scoundrel! I've got you now!' Dad exclaimed, bringing the greenhide down on the man's face, head and shoulders with a *swish, swish, swish*!

The affrighted animal pulled violently away and galloped off. A roar that surprised and startled Dad came from the man. Then there was a struggle on the grass. Dad did all the struggling. Dad was underneath. Sarah came stealthily upon the scene and, staring through the pallid night, called timidly, 'Is that you, Willie?' But when oaths mingled with sounds of violence were the only replies she received, she took alarm and fled back to the house. Billy Bearup came cantering along the lane and pulled up at the gate. Heavy kicks and gurgling and stifled cries of 'Murder! Robber! Coward!' surprised him and, wheeling around, he put spurs to his horse and broke his appointment with Sarah.

'Who the devil are you, you crawler?' the man gasped, squeezing Dad's throat. 'Speak or I'll strangle you.'

Dad gurgled out his identity and the man, who was Big Andy Daley, the butcher from Crawley's Crossing, coming to pay Dad a cheque for some bullocks, exclaimed 'Good Heavens!' and jumped off Dad and pulled him to his feet, and stared into his bruised face. 'Why, what in the name'—here he panted and puffed—'what the deuce did you mean?'

For a while Dad staggered about in the moonlight like a drunken man till he got his wind. Then he explained.

'Damn them!' Daley said, rubbing one of his eyes, which Dad had nearly cut out with the whip. 'I wish they'd made their appointment somewhere else.' And Dad agreed with Daley and sat down on the grass and spat some teeth out.

It's years ago since then, and Dad never bothers about Billy Bearup now. Neither does Sarah. Billy went to see Nellie Thompson one Sunday, and Sarah gave him up.

THE SHEARER'S SERENADE

(APOLOGY TO TENNYSON)

PIERRE CASSÉE

Come out, O Miss, from yonder homestead proud,
What I can't get inside (the shearer sang)—
Inside the shoulder cold they'd give your Bill!
So cease to live within the homestead, cease
Thy Sunbeam-soapy smiles to waste on Pa,
To stand the stare of Jackeroo Esquire;
And come and mash me in the mallee, come,
And mash me in the mallee, roll thou up
And join me on the snug selection, me,
Whose hands and lands a 'bit' will always raise,
Who never blues his cheque among the vats,
But, ant-like, saveth all, so ne'er need walk
Like snails and swaggies on their uppers borne.

Lord! The first time your ravin' locks I seen
Down dropped my heart as dropped the fleece of snow
That all about me, ringer-cloven, fell,

The tally-torrent from my dusky paws;
D'ye follow? Come, O Come, a Peg come down,
Live with me in the mallee, let the wild
Bald-headed Boss be wild (my troubles!)—leave
The crawling Jackeroo to mop and swill
And watch the smoke-wreaths from his cigarette
Fade, like his last remittance, from his sight;
So fade thou too, and come where my love-tales
Await thee; feather pillows, my sweet'eart
I'll buy for thee; my shearer calls thee, I,
I and my pipe (and sweet as it's been found
Unto my lips; sweeter thy lips would be),
Come—or, hand-hurrying like a sheep just shorn
Will issue droves from my tonsorial gums
Of really quite innumerable B's.

AN ECHO

JAMES HEPPLETHWAITE

O the wattle trees are yellowing
Adown the dark green lane,
And the bush winds are blowing so sweetly,
But I and my true love shall meet again
When I come home from the riding.

With a cooee from the mountain,
And a cooee from the vale,
With a trample and a jingle so gaily,
I call to my true love to meet me at the rail,
When I come home from the riding.

Now the she-oak leaves are sorrowing
For hearthstone cold and grey,
And my bosom is aching with sadness,
But when through the River I shall ford at close of day,
She will welcome me home from the riding.

When Miles Franklin—in truth a young 'bush girl'—wrote My Brilliant Career *in 1901, the traditional happy ending was flouted as the heroine, Sybylla, made a stand for independence. The choice between career and marriage may seem dated to today's readers, but the anguish of lovers' miscommunication remains real:*

. . . 'I am not good enough to be your wife, Hal, or that of any man. Oh, Hal, I have never deceived you! There are scores of good noble women in the world who would wed you for the asking—marry one of them.'

'But, Syb, I want you. You are the best and truest girl in the world.'

'Och! Sure, the blarney-stone is getting a good rub now,' I said playfully.

Annoyance and amusement struggled for mastery in his expression as he replied:

'You're the queerest girl in the world. One minute you snub a person, the next you are the jolliest girl going, and then you get as grave and as earnest as a fellow's mother would be.'

'Yes, I am queer. If you had any sense, you'd have nothing to do with me. I'm more queer, too. I am given to something which a man never pardons in a woman. You will draw away as though I were a snake when you hear.'

'What is it?'

'I am given to writing stories, and literary people predict I will yet be an authoress.'

He laughed—his soft, rich laugh.

'That's just into my hand. I'd rather work all day than write the shortest letter; so if you will give me a hand occasionally, you can write as many yarns as you like. I'll give you a study and send for a truck-load of writing gear at once, if you like. Is that the only horror you had to tell me?'

I bowed my head.

'Well, I can have you now,' he said gently, folding me softly in his arms with such tender reverence that I cried out in pain. 'Oh, Hal, don't don't!' and struggled free. I was ashamed, knowing I was not worthy of this.

He flushed a dusky red.

'Am I so hateful to you that you cannot bear my touch?' he asked half wistfully, half angrily.

'Oh no; it isn't that. I'm really very fond of you, if you'd only understand,' I said half to myself.

'Understand! If you care for me that is all I want to understand. I love you and have plenty of money. There is nothing to keep us apart. Now that I know you care for me, I will have you, in spite of the devil.'

'There will be a great tussle between you,' I said mischievously, laughing at him. 'Old Nick has a great hold on me, and I'm sure he will dispute your right.'

At any time Harold's sense of humour was not at all in accordance with his size, and he failed to see how my remark applied now.

He gripped my hands in a passion of pleading, as two years previously he had gripped me in jealous rage. He drew me to him. His eyes were dark and full of entreaty; his voice husky.

'Syb, poor little Syb, I will be good to you! You can have what you like. You don't know what you mean when you say no.' . . .

There was a winning charm in his manner. Nature had endowed him liberally with virile fascination. My hard ungenial life had rendered me weak. He was drawing me to him; he was irresistible. Yes; I would be his wife. I grew dizzy and turned my head sharply backwards and took a long, gasping breath, another and another, of that fresh cool air suggestive of the grand old sea and creak of cordage and bustle and strife of life. My old spirit revived, and my momentary weakness fled. There was another to think of than myself and that was Harold. Under a master-hand I would be harmless; but to this man I would be as a two-edged sword in the hand of a novice—gashing his fingers at every turn and eventually stabbing his honest heart.

It was impossible to make him see my refusal was for his good . . . He was as a favourite child pleading for a dangerous toy. I desired to gratify him, but the awful responsibility of the after-effects loomed up and deterred me.

'Hal, it can never be.'

He dropped my hands and drew himself up.

'I will not take your No till the morning. Why do you refuse me? Is it my temper? You need not be afraid of that. I don't think I'd hurt you; and I don't drink or smoke, or swear very much; and I've never destroyed a woman's name. I would not stoop to press you against your will if you were like the ordinary run of women, but you are such a queer little party, that I'm afraid you might be boggling at some funny little point that could be easily wiped out.'

'Yes, it is only a little point. But if you wipe it out you will knock the end out of the whole thing—for the point is myself. I would not suit you. It would not be wise for you to marry me.'

'But I'm the only person concerned. If you are not afraid for yourself, I am quite satisfied.'

We faced about and walked homewards in unbroken silence—too perturbed to fall into our usual custom of chewing bush-leaves as we went.

A-SHELLING PEAS

Harry (Breaker) Morant (1902)

Now, all the world is green and bright
Outside the latticed pane;
The fields are decked with gold and white,
And Spring has come again.
But though the world be fair without,
With flow'rs and waving trees,
'Tis pleasanter to be about
Where Nell's a-shelling peas.

Her eyes are blue as cloudless skies,
And dimples deck her cheeks;
Whilst soft lights loiter in her eyes
Whene'er she smiles or speaks.
So all the sunlit morning-tide
I dally at mine ease,
To loaf at slender Nelly's side
When Nell's a-shelling peas.

This bard, who sits a-watching Nell,
With fingers white and slim,
Owns up that, as she breaks each shell,
She also 'breaks up' him;
And could devoutly drop upon
Submissive, bended knees
To worship Nell with apron on—
A saint a-shelling peas.

The tucked-up muslin sleeves disclose
Her round arms white and bare—
'Tis only shelling peas that shows
Those dainty dimples there.
Old earth owns many sights to see
That captivate and please;—
The most bewitching sight for me
Is Nell a-shelling peas.

Love affairs, larrikin style, were typified by 'The Courting of Pinkey' in Louis Stone's Jonah (1911):

. . . Chook's previous love-affairs had all been conducted in the open air. Following the law of Cardigan Street, he met the girl at the street corner and spent the night in the park or the dance-room. Rarely, if she forgot the appointment, he would saunter past the house, and whistle till she came out. What passed within the house was no concern of his. Parents were his natural enemies, who regarded him with the eyes of a butcher watching a hungry dog. But his affair with Pinkey had been full of surprises, and this was not the least, that chance had given him an informal introduction to Pinkey's stepmother and the furniture.

He had called again with vegetables, and when he adroitly remarked that no one could have taken Mrs Partridge to be old enough to be the mother of Pinkey, she had spent a delightful hour leaning against the doorpost telling him how she came to marry Partridge, and the incredible number of offers she had refused in her time. Charmed with his wit and sympathy, she forgot what she was saying, and invited him to tea on the following Sunday. Chook was staggered. He knew this was the custom of the law-abiding, who nodded to the police and went to church on Sunday. But here was the fox receiving a pressing invitation from the lamb. He decided to talk the matter over with Pinkey. But when he told her of the invitation, she flushed crimson.

'She asked yous to tea, did she? The old devil!'

'W'y,' said Chook mortified.

'W'y? 'Cause she knows father'ud kill yer, if yer put yer nose inside the door.'

'Oh! would'e?' cried Chook, bristling.

'My word, yes! A bloke once came after Lil, an' 'e run 'im out so quick 'e forgot 'is 'at, an' waited at the corner till I brought it.'

'Well, 'e won't bustle me,' cried Chook.

'But y'ain't goin'?' said Pinkey, anxiously.

'My oath, I am!' cried Chook. 'I'm doin' the square thing this time, don't yous fergit, an' no old finger's goin' ter bustle me, even if 'e's your father.'

'Yous stop at 'ome while yer lucky,' said Pinkey. 'Ever since Lil cleared out wi' Marsden, 'e swears 'e'll knoife the first bloke that comes after me.'

'Ye're only kiddin',' said Chook, cheerfully; 'an' wot'll 'e do ter yous?'

'Me! 'E niver rouses on me. W'en 'e gits shirty, I just laugh, an' 'e can't keep it up.'

'Right-oh!' said Chook. 'Look out fer a song an' dance nex' Sunday.'

About five o'clock on the following Sunday afternoon, Chook, beautifully attired in the larrikin fashion, sauntered up to the door and tried the knocker. It was too stiff to move and he used his knuckles. Then he heard footsteps and a rapid whispering, and Pinkey, white with anxiety, opened the door. Mrs Partridge, half dressed, slipped into the bedroom and called out in a loud voice, 'Good afternoon, Mr Fowles! 'Ave yer come to take Elizabeth for a walk?'

Ignoring Pinkey's whispered advice, he pushed in and looked around. He was in the parlour, and a large china dog welcomed him with a fixed grin.

'W'ere's the old bloke?' muttered Chook.

Pinkey pointed to the dining-room, and Chook walked briskly in. He found Partridge in his arm-chair, scowling at him over the newspaper.

'Might I ask 'oo you are?' he growled.

'Me name's Fowles—Arthur Fowles,' replied Chook, picking a seat near the door and smoothing a crease in his hat.

'Ah! That's all I needed to know,' growled Partridge. 'Now yer can go.'

'Me? No fear!' cried Chook, affecting surprise. 'Yer missis gave me an invite ter tea an 'ere I am. Besides I ain't such a stranger as I look; I 'elped move yer furniture in.'

'An' yer shove yer way into my 'ouse on the strength of wot a pack o' silly women said ter yer?'

'I did,' admitted Chook.

'Now, you take my advice, an' git out before I break every bone in yer body.'

Chook stared at him with an unnatural stolidity for fear he would spoil everything by grinning.

'Well, wot are yer starin' at?' inquired Partridge, with irritation.

'I was wonderin' 'ow yer'd look on the end of a rope,' replied Chook quietly.

'Me on the end of a rope?' cried Partridge in amazement.

'Yes. They said yous'ud stiffen me if I cum in, an' 'ere I am.'

'An' yet you 'ad the cheek?'

'Yes,' said Chook; 'I niver take no notice o' wot women say.'

Partridge glared at him as if meditating a spring, and then, with a rapid jerk, turned his back on Chook and buried his nose in the newspaper. Pinkey and her stepmother, who were listening to this dialogue at the door, ready for flight at the first sound of breaking glass or splintered wood, now ventured to step into the room. Chook, secure of victory, criticised the weather, but Partridge remained silent as a graven image. Mrs Partridge set the table for tea with nervous haste.

'Tea's ready, William,' she cried at last.

William took his place, and, without lifting his eyes, began to serve the meat. Mrs Partridge had made a special effort. She had bought a pig's cheek, some German sausage, and a dozen scones at seven for threepence. This was flanked by bread-and-butter, and a newly opened tin of jam with the jagged lid of the tin standing upright. She thought, with pride, that the young man would see he was in a house where no expense was spared. She requested Chook to sit next to Pinkey and talked with feverish haste.

'Which do yer like, Mr Fowles? Lean or fat? The fat sometimes melts in yer mouth. Give 'im that bit yer cut for me, William.'

'If 'e don't like it, 'e can leave it,' growled Partridge.

'Now, that'll do, William. I always said yer bark was worse than yer bite. You'll be all right w'en yer've 'ad yer beer. 'E's got the temper of an angel w'en 'e's 'ad 'is beer,' she explained to Chook, as if her husband was out of hearing.

Partridge sat with his eyes fixed on his plate with the face of a sulky schoolboy. His long features reminded Chook of a horse he had once driven. When he had finished eating, he pulled his chair back and buried his silly, obstinate face in the newspaper. He had evidently determined to ignore Chook's existence. Mrs Partridge broke the silence by describing his character to the visitor as if he were a naughty child.

'William always sulks w'en 'e can't get 'is own way. Not another word will we 'ear from 'im tonight. 'E knows 'e ought to be civil to people as eat at 'is own table, an' that only makes 'im worse. But for all 'is sulks, 'e's got the temper of an angel w'en 'e's 'ad 'is beer. I've met all sorts—them as smashes the furniture for spite an' them as bashes their wives 'cause it's cheaper, but gimme William every time.'

Partridge took no notice, except to bury his nose deeper in the paper. He had reached the advertisements, and a careful study of these would carry him safely to bed. After tea, Pinkey set to work and washed up the dishes, while Mrs Partridge entertained the guest. Chook took out his cigarettes and asked if Mr Partridge objected to smoke. There was no answer.

'You must speak louder, Mr Fowles,' said Mrs Partridge. 'William's 'earing ain't wot it used to be.'

William resented this remark by twisting his chair further away and emitting a grunt.

Pinkey, conscious of Chook's eyes, was bustling in and out with the airs of a busy housewife, her arms, thin as a broomstick, bared to the elbow. His other love-affairs had belonged to the open air, with the street for a stage and the park for scenery, and this domestic setting struck him as a novelty. Pinkey, then, was not merely a plaything for an hour, but a woman of serious uses, like the old mother who suckled him and would hear no ill word of him. And as he watched with greedy eyes the animal died within him, and a sweeter emotion than he had ever known filled his ignorant, passionate heart. For the first time in his life he understood why men gave up their pals and the freedom of the streets for a woman. Mrs Partridge saw the look in his eyes, and wished she were twenty years younger. When Pinkey got her hat and proposed a walk, Chook softened by his novel emotions, called out 'Good night, boss!'

For a wonder, Partridge looked up from his paper and grunted 'Night!'

'There now!' cried Mrs Partridge, delighted, 'William wouldn't say that to everybody, would you William? Call again any time you like, an' 'e'll be in a better temper.'

When they reached the park, they sat on a seat facing the asphalt path. Near them was another pair, the donah, with a hat like a tea-tray, nursing her bloke's head in her lap as he lay full length along the seat. And they exchanged caresses with a royal indifference to the people who were sauntering along the paths. But, without knowing why, Chook and Pinkey sat as far apart as if they had freshly studied a book on etiquette. For to Chook, this fair girl with the bronze hair and shabby clothes was no longer a mere donah, but a laborious housewife and a potential mother of children; and to Pinkey this was a new Chook, who kept his hands to himself, and looked at her with eyes that made her forget she was a poor factory girl . . .

ACTRESS LOTTIE LYELL AND DIRECTOR RAYMOND LONGFORD BECAME LOVERS AND FORMED A CREATIVE PARTNERSHIP, PRODUCING THE CLASSIC CINEMATIC VERSION OF *THE SENTIMENTAL BLOKE*. ALTHOUGH AS 'DOREEN' LOTTIE LIVED HAPPILY EVER AFTER IN THE FILM, HER OWN LIFE WAS CUT TRAGICALLY SHORT WHEN SHE DIED OF TUBERCULOSIS AT THE AGE OF THIRTY-SIX. LONGFORD HAD BEEN UNABLE TO MARRY LOTTIE, AS HE COULD NOT DIVORCE HIS CATHOLIC WIFE. HOWEVER, WHEN HE DIED THIRTY YEARS LATER HIS FAMILY AGREED TO HIS EXTRAORDINARY REQUEST THAT HE BE BURIED WITH HIS LOVER AND A MONUMENT WAS ERECTED TO BOTH OF THEM.

LOVE'S COMING

JOHN SHAW NEILSON (1911)

Quietly as rosebuds
Talk to the thin air,
Love came so lightly
I knew not he was there.

Quietly as lovers
Creep at the middle moon
Softly as players tremble
In the tears of a tune;

Quietly as lilies
Their faint vows declare
Came the sky pilgrim:
I knew not he was there.

Quietly as tears fall
On a wild sin
Softly as griefs call
In a violin;

Without hail or tempest
Blue sword or flame,
Love came so lightly
I knew not that he came.

Teach me not, tell me not,
Love ever sinned!
See how her petticoat
Sweetens the wind.

JOHN SHAW NEILSON
'The Petticoat Plays'

Harold Cazneaux 1878–1953, *Winifred Cazneaux*, 1906

As author of the passionate 'My Country', Dorothea MacKellar could reasonably be expected to have had similar tone in her personal life. This was not the case, however, and stubborn Dorothea is thought to have died virgo intacta many years after a silly misunderstanding ended her hopes of marriage to English banker Patrick Chalmers.

Dorothea met the well-to-do young man when she travelled to England in 1914. After their first dinner together, she scribbled cryptically in her diary that she ' . . . couldn't sleep for excitement at seeing him—and other reasons'. Chalmers asked Dorothea to marry him a few days before she embarked on her return voyage, and she promised him an answer as soon as she arrived in Australia, duly sending him a letter after conferring with her parents. Poor Dorothea was to receive no answer to her letter and, after three lonely years, heard he had married another girl. The final twist of the knife came when, on meeting her ex-lover, she found he had never received her letter as the ship carrying it had been sunk by Germans.

LOOKING FORWARD

DOROTHEA MACKELLAR

What shall I do, my darling, when
implacable Spring comes by again
With birdsong and boronia's breath
And sure to me as man's sure death
The knowledge that your love is gone—
What shall I stay my heart upon?

Where shall I turn to hide from you?
Little red leaf-buds sticky-new,
And busy blue wrens that trail a stem
Of couchgrass eagerly after them,
Every knot of Spring's silk mesh
Must bind my heart to pain afresh.

Eastward through scents and sounds that ache
With sweetness of honey in bush and brake
Blindly I'll turn me, hastening
Towards the sea that knows no spring,
And where the indifferent combers roll
Bathe mind and body and desperate soul.

Salt of our blood and tears is kin
To salt of the sea that watched life begin:
Her cold voice is less fell than earth's
Harlequin round of deaths and births
And loves containing each: in her
Perhaps I shall find a comforter.

What shall I do when Spring comes by.
Love being dead? I shall not cry
To you, but, till my eyes are clear,
I'll turn my back on the sweet of the year.
We share no memories of the sea . . .
You nearly could be proud of me.

L. Hey Sharp 1885–1965, *Melbourne*, 1929

THE ELECTRIC TRAM TO KEW

LESBIA HARFORD (1915)

Through the swift night
I go to my love.
Tram bells are joy bells,
Bidding us move
On a golden path
Beneath balls of fire
Up hill and down dale,
To o'ertake desire.

Past the old shops
That my childhood knew,
Past hidden houses
And fields of dew
Lovely and secret
As thou, my friend,
Who art all heaven
At journey's end.

AUSTRALIAN ABORIGINES ATE THE PHALLIC STINKHORN FUNGUS IN THE BELIEF IT WOULD MAKE THEM BETTER LOVERS, ALTHOUGH ITS SMELL IS PRETTY APPALLING. FAR PREFERABLE IS THE PITTOSPORUM TREE: MEN CRUSHED THE SEEDS AND PLACED THEM NEAR THE WOMEN'S SHELTERS, AS THE POWERFUL AROMA WAS SAID TO DRIVE THE WOMEN CRAZY WITH DESIRE. IF THAT FAILED, THE MEN WOULD SMEAR THEIR CHESTS WITH A PASTE MADE OF FAIRY PAINTBRUSH BARK AND CHARCOAL. INTERESTINGLY, THE AUSTRALIAN LEAFLESS MISTLETOE WAS ONCE REGARDED AS A LOVE-INDUCING PLANT IN MUCH THE SAME WAY AS ITS EUROPEAN COUSIN WAS.

THE PLAY
C. J. DENNIS (1915)

'Wot's in a name?' she sez . . . An' then she sighs,
An' clasps 'er little 'ands, an' rolls 'er eyes.
'A rose,' she sez, 'be any other name
Would smell the same.
Oh, w'erefore art you Romeo, young sir?
Chuck yer ole pot, an' change yer moniker!'

Doreen an' me, we bin to see a show—
The swell two-dollar touch. Bong tong, yeh know.
A chair apiece wiv velvit on the seat;
A slap-up treat.
The drarmer's writ be Shakespeare, years ago,
About a barmy goat called Romeo.

'Lady, be yonder moon I swear!' sez 'e.
An' then 'e climbs up on the balkiney;
An' there they smooge a treat, wiv pretty words
Like two love-birds.
I nudge Doreen. She whispers, 'Ain't it grand!'
'Er eyes is shinin'; an' I squeeze 'er 'and.

'Wot's in a name?' she sez. 'Struth, I dunno.
Billo is just as good as Romeo.
She may be Juli–er or Juli–et—
'E loves 'er yet.
If she's the tart 'e wants, then she's 'is queen,
Names never count . . . But ar, I like 'Doreen'!

A sweeter, dearer sound I never 'eard;
Ther's music 'angs around that little word,
Doreen! . . . But wot was this I starts to say
About the play?
I'm off me beat. But when a bloke's in love
'Is thorts turn 'er way, like a 'omin' dove.

This Romeo 'e's lurkin' wiv a crew—
A dead tough crowd o' crooks—called Montague.
'Is cliner's push—wot's nicknamed Capulet—
They 'as 'em set.
Fair narks they are, jist like them back-street clicks,
Ixcep' they fights wiv skewers 'stid o' bricks.

Wot's in a name? Wot's in a string o' words?
They scraps in ole Verona wiv the'r swords,
An' never give a bloke a stray dog's chance,
An' that's Romance.
But when they deals it out wiv bricks an' boots
In Little Lon., they're low, degraded broots.

Wot's jist plain stoush wiv us, right 'ere to-day,
Is 'valler' if yer fur enough away.
Some time, some writer bloke will do the trick
Wiv Ginger Mick,
Of Spadger's Lane. 'E'll be a Romeo,
When 'e's bin dead five 'undred years or so.

Fair Juli–et, she gives 'er boy the tip.
Sez she: 'Don't sling that crowd o' mine no lip;
An' if you run agin a Capulet,
Jist do a get.'
'E swears 'e's done wiv lash; 'e'll chuck it clean.
(Same as I done when I first met Doreen).

They smooge some more at that. Ar, strike me blue!
It gimme Joes to sit an' watch them two!
'E'd break away an' start to say goodbye,
An' then she'd sigh
'Ow, Ro-me-o!' an' git a strangle-holt,
An' 'ang around 'im like she feared 'e'd bolt.

Nex' day 'e words a gorspil cove about
A secrit weddin'; an' they plan it out.
'E spouts a piece about 'ow 'e's bewitched:

Then they git 'itched . . .
Now, 'ere's the place where I fair git the pip:
She's 'is for keeps, an' yet 'e lets 'er slip!

Ar! but 'e makes me sick! A fair gazob!
'E's jist the glarsey on the soulful sob,
'E'll sigh and spruik an' 'owl a love-sick vow—
(The silly cow!)
But when 'e's got 'er, spliced an' on the straight,
'E crools the pitch, an' tries to kid it's Fate.

Aw! Fate me foot! Instid of slopin' soon
As 'e was wed, off on 'is 'oneymoon,
'Im an' 'is cobber, called Mick Curio,
They 'ave to go
An' mix it wiv that push o' Capulets.
They look fer trouble; an' it's wot they gets

A tug named Tyball (cousin to the skirt)
Sprags 'em an' makes a start to sling off dirt.
Nex' minnit there's a reel ole ding-dong go—
'Arf round or so.
Mick Curio, 'e gets it in the neck,
'Ar rats!' 'e says, an' passes in 'is check.

Quite natchril, Romeo gits wet as 'ell.
'It's me or you!' 'e 'owls, an' wiv a yell,
Plunks Tyball through the gizzard wiv 'is sword,
'Ow I ongcored!
'Put in the boot!' I sez. 'Put in the boot!'
''Ush!' sez Doreen . . . 'Shame!' sez some silly coot.

Then Romeo, 'e dunno wot to do.
The cops git busy, like they allwiz do,
An' nose around until 'e gits blue funk
An' does a bunk.
They wants 'is tart to wed some other guy.
'Ah, strike!' she sez. 'I wish that I could die!'

Now, this 'ere gorspil bloke's a fair shrewd 'ead.
Sez 'e, 'I'll dope yeh, so they'll *think* yer dead.'
(I tips 'e was a cunnin' sort, wot knoo
A thing or two.)
She takes 'is knock-out drops, up in 'er room:
They think she's snuffed, an' plant 'er in 'er tomb.

Then things get mixed a treat an' starts to whirl.
'Ere's Romeo comes back an' finds 'is girl
Tucked in 'er little coffing, cold an' stiff,
An' in a jiff,
'E swallers lysol, throws a fancy fit,
'Ead over turkey, an' 'is soul 'as flit.

Then Juli–et wakes up an' sees 'im there,
Turns on the water-works an' tears 'er 'air,
'Dear love,' she sez, 'I cannot live alone!'
An', wiv a moan,
She grabs 'is pockit knife, an' ends 'er cares . . .
'*Peanuts or lollies*!' sez a boy upstairs.

Confident, young and innocent, thousands of Australian men enlisted to fight in the Great War of 1914–18. High hopes of adventure were swiftly replaced by serious consideration that they might never return home. Final letters written to wives and sweethearts on the eve of the Anzac landing in 1915 still touch the heart:

Well Darling one at 12 o'clock tonight . . . we go over the parapet and then our fate is sealed—if I am lucky we'll be relieved within a week . . . The place is like Hell darling but the sooner we get it over the better . . . remember it is better to die for you and country than to be a cheat of the empire. I'll try love for your sake to do well and come through . . . God be with you Love for all Time . . . Remember me to Baby when she is Born—if a boy don't make him a tin soldier but should war break out let him enlist and do his bit if not he'll be no son of mine.

CAPTAIN A. McLEOD OF KATANNING, WA
(AGED TWENTY-FIVE AND FIVE MONTHS MARRIED)

. . . I trust that I will come through alright, but it is impossible to say, and I must do my duty whatever it is. But if I am to die, know that I died loving you . . . if in some future time, you should think of remarrying, always know that I would wish you to do whatever is for your own happiness. But think well, dear, and make sure what manner of man you take . . .

MAJOR B.B.LANE OF PROSPECT, SA
(AGED TWENTY-SEVEN YEARS)

Dear Gladys, there is a little matter. We are about to take part in some very severe fighting and there is no doubt that those who come through it alive will be very lucky. If I should go under there is no need for me to say of whom my last thoughts will be . . . I hope you will always remain on the best of terms with my mother and the others and if in the years to come to require genuine friends you can rely on finding them among my family . . . Mere written words could not convey my feelings regarding you dearest, I know that you know, and that is sufficient.

SERGEANT M.J. RANFORD, OF SEMAPHORE, SA
(AGED THIRTY-FIVE)

Katharine Susannah Prichard's one great love was Hugo ('Jim') Throssel. She records his return in 1918 from the war in her diary:

He stood at the foot of the stairs, a tall, masterful figure in uniform— returned from the maelstrom of war—my irresolution vanished. He held out his arms and I walked down the stairs into them.

They were married in 1919 and she was to write to a friend:

My husband is truly, I believe, the best thing that ever happened to me
. . . We lived in only two or three rooms and on hot summer evenings
disported ourselves like Adam and Eve in the garden. During those
honeymoon months I gave Jim Engel's *Socialism, Utopian and Scientific* to
read. As he sprawled over it on the verandah, often there would be a
yell of: 'Hell, girl, what the blazes does this mean?' I would go out to
explain, his arms stretch out, and usually our political discussion ended
in love-making.

One of Prichard's most tender poems was titled, simply, 'To Jim':

> To you, all these wild weeds
> and windflowers of my life,
> I bring, my lord,
> and lay them at your feet;
> They are not frankincense
> or myrrh,
> but you are Krishna, Christ and Dionysos
> in your beauty, tenderness and strength.

JUST TO DRIFT
RODERIC QUINN (1920)

Drifting down the Harbour,
Stars on high,
Lovers of the surface,
You and I,
Let us never pry and wonder
At the things that lie thereunder.

Underneath the surface
Silver-fair,
Let us never question
What lies there;
Lest we lose, like some robbed miser,
All our treasure, growing wiser.

Lo, it has the beauty
Of a flower!
Is it not sufficient
For the hour
Just to drift as mists are drifted,
Depths unplumbed and veils unlifted?

Where's the flawless jewel,
Stainless breast?
Where's the Love that answers
Every test?
Where's the past that's altogether
Cloudless as this radiant weather?

Drifting down the Harbour
On the tide,
Careless of all knowledge,
Let us glide,
Heedless of what Life discovers,
Save that you and I are lovers.

397., THE OLD WHARF, MOSMAN'S BAY.

In Mary Grant Bruce's final Billabong book, Billabong's Daughter, *an episode with a roan bull finally precipitated true love between Norah and Wally, much to the satisfaction of a generation of Australian readers:*

. . . He flung himself down from his horse, his face white.
'Norah—you're all right?'
She nodded; unable to speak for a moment, smiling at him. 'Thanks

to you. He—he'd have had me but for you, Wally.'

'I thought I'd never get here in time,' Wally said, his voice shaking. 'It was Garryowen I saw first, just as I topped the rise, and I thought I'd better hurry back—I knew something was wrong. And then I saw you run out. Norah—Norah, I never thought I'd be in time!'

The agony in his voice made her forget her own fear.

'But you were,' she said. 'Nobody else would have come so quickly, I believe.'

'It seemed about the longest ride I ever took,' said Wally. He put out his hand towards her; then it dropped to his side and he stood staring at her. 'I—I can hardly believe yet you're safe.' He pulled himself together, drawing a long breath. 'I must get after that brute and yard him,' he said, commanding his voice with an effort . . . 'Sure you're all right, Nor? Not feeling shaky?'

'Is it me?' asked Norah, in the voice of Mary-Kate. 'Sure I am not.'

'Then I'll be leaving you to get on with me job, or your brother will ate the face off me!' returned he merrily. 'You can't meet any more bulls because there are no more to meet. I can see your mates: Tommy is on that ridge to the north and Bob on the spur beyond that; they're both bringing down cattle.'

'Than I'd better get busy or they'll think I'm slacking,' Norah said practically. She met Wally's eyes with a little smile; somehow it did not seem so easy as usual. But that was, of course, nonsense. It was enough to make anyone upset, to have seen Wally so queer and white and shaken—Wally, who made a joke of everything.

RED HAT
LESBIA HARFORD (1919)

I bought a red hat
To please my lover.
He will hardly see it
When he looks me over,
Though it's a fine hat.
Yet he never misses
Noticing my red mouth
When it's shaped for kisses.

BECAUSE SHE WOULD ASK ME WHY I LOVED HER

CHRISTOPHER BRENNAN (1923)

If questioning could make us wise
no eyes would ever gaze in eyes;
if all our tale were told in speech
no mouths would wander each to each.

Were spirits free from mortal mesh
and love not bound in hearts of flesh
no aching breasts would yearn to meet
and find their ecstasy complete.

For who is there that lives and knows
the secret powers by which he grows?
Were knowledge all, what were our need
to thrill and faint and sweetly bleed?

Then seek not, sweet, the *If* and *Why*
I love you now until I die:
For I must love because I live
and life in me is what you give.

The wedding of May Gibbs, mother of Australia's dearly loved gumnut babies Snugglepot and Cuddlepie, did not go unnoticed by the press. The Perth Ladies Sphere *reported in 1919 that:*

Quite lately . . . a curious phenomenon was observed. Just above roof level a cloud of diaphanous insects was seen all hurrying in the same direction. One dropped exhausted out of the throng to lie, golden brown and gasping, on the pavement. He was a gumnut baby, curvy, fat and wreathed and capped in orange blossom.

To anxious questions he replied nothing; jumping into a taxi, he sped away to join the cloud of his brothers and sisters. They hovered in a song around her head, while May Gibbs was being made Mrs James Ossoli Kelly. When the ceremony was over they flew back, still singing, into the bush. The marriage was celebrated quietly on Thursday.

The independent and feisty Miss Gibbs—or Mrs Kelly, as she was by then—left her publisher speechless when she finally answered their frantic letters of inquiry:

. . . I've *not* given you the autographed Snug and Cud, and I did *not* write the nice letter to Mr Robertson that I intended to—but I got married! It needs no further explanation or excuse, does it? . . .

LOVE IS NOT LOVE
LESBIA HARFORD(1925)

When I was still a child
I thought my love would be
Noble, truthful, brave,
And very kind to me.

Then all the words said
That if my lover prove
No such man as this
He had to forfeit love.

Now I know life holds
Harder tasks in store.
If my lover fails
I must love him more.

Should he prove unkind,
What am I, that he
Squander soul and strength
Smoothing life for me?

Weak or false or cruel
Love must still be strong.
All my life I'll learn
How to love as long.

John Shaw Neilsen's 'Her Eyes Foretold of Happiness' (1924) may have had a romantic secret. It seems Neilsen was very impressed by fellow poet Mary Gilmore and said to her: 'I'll see if I can't write a bit of verse for you,' before sending her this piece, tentatively subtitled 'For Mary Gilmore'. Gruff publisher A. G. Stephens was 'a little offended that I hadn't sent it to him first' and left out the dedication when it was printed.

Her eyes foretold of happiness
As grapes foretell of wine;
Her feet were like the light that falls
In greeneries divine.

Her forehead seemed a clear heaven
Where all the loves agree;
Her lips were like the flowers' lips
So delicate was she.

Her hair was like a joy that walks
In a long fallen rhyme;
Her bosom was a white morning
In the keen Summer-time.

Oh, lips that lightly gave and gave
The laugh to Jeopardy!
I know not how about the world
So sweet a mouth could be.

ENDEAVOURING TO FORGET HIS MOTHER'S TRAGIC SUICIDE, MAVERICK
COMPOSER AND MUSICIAN PERCY GRAINGER SAILED FROM AUSTRALIA TO
EUROPE IN 1926 ABOARD THE *AORANGI*. THERE HE MET THE BEAUTIFUL AND
PHLEGMATIC ELLA STROM, WHO AT FIRST MISTOOK HIM FOR THE SHIP'S
PIANIST. ON THEIR BETROTHAL PERCY COMMENTED:

After the great spiritual cut-off-ness and loneliness I have borne since the
death of my beloved mother, it is an unspeakable boon to me to have this
soul satisfying comrade to me to commune with and to look forward to
sharing my life with in so near a future . . . Miss Strom is the very
prototype of radiant Nordic, as lovely as the morning to look upon and a
regular Amazon to walk, run, swim and dance and play games.

FOR THE WEDDING CEREMONY HE COMPOSED A SPECIAL SONG, 'TO MY
NORDIC PRINCESS', AND CLAIMED HE LOVED HER ALL HIS LIFE. EVEN AT AGE
SEVENTY-SEVEN HE WROTE:

My own heart's dearest, bewitching Ella, I think both you and I are
unusually gentle and subtle and therefore I consider it a miracle of good
luck that we met and wedded . . . I am so endlessly thankful to my
darling wife.

Sydney Long 1871–1955, *By Tranquil Waters*, 1894

LOVE PHILTRE
KATHARINE SUSANNAH PRICHARD

'Cure your soul through your sense,
Or your senses through your soul?'

Beloved—
If all my wit and witchcraft will avail,
A philtre I will brew which cannot fail
you of the mystery.

I'll gather musk and dogwood, after rain,
Pennyroyal, too,
Wild hops, centaury and sassafras,
Points of grass, green as grasshopper
who preys upon them,
Blood of tall trees and buds of saplings,

The leaf a butterfly alighted on—
A golden winged, ringed *Xenica*,
With owl's head etched beneath his wing—
Honey dripping blossom of the sugar gum
which bees and ants love,
And little birds who sing with faint sweet tinklings
as of silver bells, have nests among.

All, all in creekwater,
Clear as dew, I'll strew,
And wander further, murmuring spells,
and incantations to the sun and moon and stars:
Forces of earth and air,
Of light and darkness, wind and rain,
The secret sources of a fecund soil,
Of life and death, and joy and pain.

A thread of stringy bark with ferns and moss,
Wild violets and maiden hair
Fey light has run its fingers through,
I'll shred, with wood of a dead tree
That yellow fungi feed upon,
In whose dark spores the vermilion spider breeds,
Infinitesimal as dust, and evil as all ill.
Of every seed I'll gather one
And hold it to the midday sun,
So that their fruitfulness will mingle with your mirth
And all your sorrows die in throes of birth.

From thickets where the thrush has sung,
I'll take a wattle spray,
And seek the twig a yellow robin
tuned his harp notes in the dawn upon,
And bid it yield the melody its sap drew in.
Wild heath, pink flushing as the morning sky,
And tetratheca, mauve and blue of distant hills,
I'll take and break, and tell them
That they grew for you.

Orchids and insects,
Weeds that lace-winged flies have spread
their wings and shimmered over,
The living sapphire of a tiny bug,
beetles enamelled green and blue, and gold, and bronze,
A caul of spring, and fragments from the shroud of autumn,
Seeds, chrysalis, ore, bark and buds,
Honey and manna;
Mushrooms pushing through red loam,
Flowers, pink, purple, yellow, brown and white,
from all the hills;
Shadow and mists,
The smoke of forest fires,
Needles of summer showers . . .

And as stars bloom in the twilight sky,
All these I'll take and press their virtue from,
Holding to simmer over my heart's ember,
With masses to the genii of the earth and air,
And secret oaths to all the spirits of the past and future,
Silene, Hecate, Prometheus and the Brotherhood of Man.

Then, if you come, I'll fill that beaker,
Shaped after the body of the first woman,
To offer you the potion I have made;
And when you've drained my brew,
Invoking every element of life and death,
The god will rise in you.
Upon an ecstasy of soul confounding sense,
Soul will be senses, senses soul.
And so, my cure be proved:
Or—that you do not love, Beloved.

When Coonardoo was published in 1929, author Katharine Susannah Prichard had
to include a preface saying the novel was simply a work of imagination. 'Facts,
characters and incidents have been collected, related and interwoven, that is all.' This
justification is less odd when we consider the mores of the time: the Australian public

considered love between a white man and a black woman completely unacceptable, fictitious or not.

The scene where the young girl Coonardoo follows her master Hugh to muster strayed cattle probably caused most of the furore:

She was like his own soul riding there, dark, passionate and childlike. In all this wide empty world Coonardoo was the only living thing he could speak to, Hugh knew; the only creature who understood what he was feeling, and was feeling for him. Yet he was afraid of her, resented a secret understanding between them.

But Coonardoo the playmate—Coonardoo whom he had seen long ago under the shower, young and slender, her lithe brown body, wet and gleaming, brown eyes laughing at him, her hair, wavy and sun-burnished, lying in wet streaks about her head. Coonardoo? Why should he hurt her by a harsh, indifferent manner he showed no one else?

It had been funny to find her one of Warieda's women with a kid of her own when he came home from school. But sentimental about a gin Hugh had promised himself never to be. His regard for Coonardoo was a relic of their old playmateship, his admiration of her horsemanship.

Every finer, less reasonable instinct he had stamped on, kicked out of his consciousness.

'What's the matter with you?' he asked roughly as he came up to her, leaning against her horse. 'Warieda beat you?'

'Wiah.' She looked at him with deep, beautiful eyes . . .

Hugh sat down again. A trembling seized him. He had a swift vision of passion and tenderness stalking him through all the lonely misery of his wandering. When he looked up he saw Coonardoo was still standing there in the shadow.

'Sit down,' he said. And a moment later, 'You must be tired too. We've come a long way, Coonardoo?'

She nodded and sank down on the earth at a little distance from him. Her fingers, as a matter of course, went after the sticks lying about; they piled leaves and twigs. Hugh struck a match and set a flame spurting over the leaves and sticks. He saw then how tired she was, her body sagged; she was half asleep already as she sat beside the fire.

'We'll rest here a bit,' Hugh said. 'Then you can show me the way to camp again, Coonardoo.'

She nodded, smiled and stretched to sleep on the far side of the fire. Hugh sat watching her. Years fell away between them. She was Coonardoo, the old playmate; he felt about her as he had when they were children together. This was a childish adventure they were on. His gratitude shook him as he thought of how she had followed and watched over him during the last weeks. It yielded to yearning and tenderness. Deep inexplicable currents of his being flowed towards her.

'Coonardoo! Coonardoo!' he murmured.

Awakened, she came to kneel beside him, her eyes the fathomless shining of a well in the shadows. Hugh took her in his arms, and gave himself to the spirit which drew him, from a great distance it seemed, to the common source which was his life and Coonardoo's.

They slept beside the fire near the clump of dead mulga until it was morning. Hugh started up to find Coonardoo stirring embers on the fire. They had walked back into the camp then.

'Lost me tracks. Was fair bushed when Coonardoo found me,' Hugh told the boys. No more was said of the matter.

The partnership between Joe and Enid Lyons began when the thirty-five-year-old State Education Minister met and fell in love with the seventeen-year-old teacher. They shared marriage, twelve children and a political crisis that split a party and a nation. Nothing diminished their love and when Joe became Prime Minister in 1932 he wrote to Enid:

Whatever honours or distinction come are *ours*, not mine! Girl, we've seen some changes and we've lived full lives in our years of married life, and it is grand to know that our love for each other is still our most cherished and valued possession. It has grown sweeter and more beautiful with the years and with God's help it will still go on increasing as the years come and go . . . It has been a great day for me, but I would be happier on the Hill [their home in Devonport] with you and all the children . . .

Author and ardent Communist Kylie Tennant married fellow 'Red' Lewis Rodd, or 'Roddy', in 1932. In typically crusty fashion, she reminisced about the courtship:

It was of course, obligatory among radicals to sleep with whomever you intended to marry so I slept with Roddy on the bank of the Castlereagh in the moonlight. Very romantic, but by bad luck a moth got into my ear. It flutted [sic] and whirred and took all my attention. I did not think it would be polite to say: 'Could you stop seducing me because I have a moth in my ear?' So I carried on, doing my best. The damned moth continued whirring and keeping me awake in the so-called romantic moonlight long after Roddy had gone to sleep. Some people, I thought glumly, might think that moth was trying to warn me. Whenever I have presented to me what might look like an evil omen I immediately do whatever anyone sensible might be warned against—for instance, by a moth in their ear. When we were cooking breakfast over a campfire and Roddy was picking grass seeds out of his trousers I said thoughtfully: 'Roddy, what about marrying me?'

'Done,' Roddy responded promptly and began making plans about the ceremony. I reflected that if I didn't find it satisfactory I could always divorce him. After all, I had only known him on committees.

Sidney Kidman, better known as Australia's 'cattle king', could be described as the greatest pastoral landholder in modern history. His marriage to Bel was a very happy one. In 1935, his dry bushman's wit surfaced when he was asked during an interview on cattle pricing and the market what he considered to be the greatest deal he'd ever made. With a twinkle, he replied: 'My wife. She's been my mate for fifty years.'

THE RELATIONSHIP BETWEEN AUTHOR HENRY HANDEL RICHARDSON AND HER HUSBAND, JOHN G. ROBERTSON, CONTINUED BEYOND THE GRAVE. THEY WERE INTELLECTUALLY VERY COMPATIBLE AND HE WAS AN EXTREMELY DILIGENT PROOF READER OF HER WORK. WHEN HE DIED IN 1933 SHE WAS DEVASTATED BY THE LOSS OF HER CLOSEST COMPANION. DESPITE HIS DEATH SHE REFUSED TO ACCEPT THAT SHE COULD NO LONGER COMMUNICATE WITH HIM. THUS, SHE RESUMED HER RELATIONSHIP WITH HIM THROUGH SEANCES AND THE OUIJA-BOARD. SHE PLAYED MUSIC TO HIM, READ TO HIM AND TOLD HIM OF HER DIFFICULTIES WITH WRITING. WHEN SHE DIED FROM CANCER IN 1946 HER ASHES WERE SCATTERED, WITH THE ASHES OF HER HUSBAND, INTO THE SEA. SHE WANTED HER INTIMACY WITH HIM TO NOT ONLY GO BEYOND HIS DEATH BUT ALSO BEYOND HERS.

And his lids, which had fallen to again, made one last supreme effort to rise, and this time there was no mistaking the whisper that came over his lips.

'Dear wife!'

He was gone again, even as he said it, but it was enough...more than enough!...Eternity was something vast, cold, impersonal. But this little phrase, from the long past days of love and comradeship, these homely, familiar words, fell like balsam on her heart. All his love for her, his gratitude to her, was in them: they were her reward, and a full and ample one, for a lifetime of unwearied sacrifice.

THE FORTUNES OF RICHARD MAHONEY

By 1930, romance was a way of avoiding the dreary reality of the economic depression that gripped Australia. Kenneth Slessor referred to this escapism from 'the cruel fiscal realities preached by Sir Otto Niemeyer' in his 'Night of Romance'.

Let Banks and Bailiffs rule the land—
Oh, what do lovers care?
The tide still floats upon the sand,
The moon still rules the air.

The sky is still with magic blent,
The heart still cries a tune—
Who'll cut the night by Ten Per Cent,
And who can tax the moon?

A tram is cheap, a kiss is free,
Whate'er the bank proposes;
We'll swap our Otto £ s d
For 'Otto' made from roses!

Teens was possibly Australia's most famous school girl novel. In Teens Triumphant *(1933), the last book of the series, heroine Lennie Leighton falls in love with another expatriot whilst travelling in Europe:*

He tightened his hold on her. She shut her eyes. She shrank closer to his breast. Italy vanished, castle, palaces, cathedrals and all. Even the poem of distant purple Vallombrosa dissolved and was no more, and the cypress-trees flew into oblivion, and the beloved traditions of the Cinquecento passed into utter nothingness and the spell of London came to an end.

In that fond hour the two Australians found on each other's lips only their native land.

They saw only the dear old Australian bush waving its beauties at them with necromantic guile. All the dear old familiar scents stole over them, clasped in each other's arms on the Tuscan hillside. Together they smelled again the dear old yellow wattle, the dear old white ineffable pittosporum, the dear old brown boronia, the dear old perfume of burning gum-trees and ants that is as truly Australian as coffee and chestnuts is truly Paris. Again, the dear old Murrumbidgee, the dear old Darling, the dear old Murray, the dear old Hawkesbury, the dear old Hunter, the dear old Clarence, the dear old Yarra flashed over the dear old boundless Monaro and Riverina, unrolling magically before their closed eyes . . . And over all flowed the laughter of the dear old kookaburras

. . . and the dauntless spirit of the dear old Australians who lived out there: the bravest, the gayest, the cleverest, yet the most childlike and happy-go-lucky people left on earth, so they seemed to the lovers clasped in each other's arms on the Tuscan hillside . . .

Even when their big blue car was rushing along by the moonlit Mediterranean, drawing nearer and nearer to Naples and their ship, they kept hurling the dear old names at each other through the Italian night and Carlo, who had been whisked off as companion to the driver, thought the strange sounds were poems they were saying, these *forestieri*; the poetry of England, he artlessly took them to be, as the sounds floated into his muffled ears.

'Murrurundi!'

'Murwillumbah!'

'Goondiwindi!'

'Collarenebri!'

'Onkaparinka!'

'Cunnamulla!'

But we whose hearts 'remember how', we know, that they were just the dear old Australian names flung out towards each other across the breaking down in their sudden delirious abandonment to the great Whistler's tenet:

No man should remain away too long from his own country.

Tip Kelaher wrote 'The Digger Hat' and other verses while stationed in the Middle East with the AIF Machine Gun Battalion. Killed in action in 1942, his poems described an Australia of cricket, bush picnics, surf beaches, blue gums and mateship now fading into nostalgia:

> The smell of salt on a fresh sea breeze,
> Day dies and the light grows dim,
> While up on the point the tall pine trees
> Are sighing their evening hymn.
> The lights glow out on the concrete street
> Where the shop fronts face the sea,
> But where a boy and his young love meet
> The night is cool and free.

Your eyes are shining, my love, my love,
With the old, old haunting light—
I'd give my chance of Heaven above
To hold you again tonight,
With the scattered clouds and the moon above,
The sand and the wind-blown spray.
Why do I think of you now, old love,
Long buried and far away?

WILLIAM CHARLES WENTWORTH HAD A MARVELLOUS GIFT FOR THE UNCONVENTIONAL. IN 1935, HE PROPOSED TO HIS FUTURE WIFE OVER THE TELEPHONE; ACCORDING TO SYDNEY NEWSPAPERS, IT WAS THE LONGEST TELEPHONE CALL ON RECORD. TO ADD INSULT TO AN ALREADY INJURIOUS TELEPHONE BILL, WENTWORTH MADE THE PROPOSAL WHEN HIS BRIDE-TO-BE, BARBARA CHISHOLM BAIRD OF MONA VALE, WAS VISITING MEXICO.

Despite the cynicism he adopted when writing of love for Sydney's Daily Telegraph *and* Smith's Weekly *from the late 1930s to his death in 1947, Lennie Lower was always affectionate to his own wife, Phyllis. Without Fleas—as he dubbed her—life wasn't worth living:*

NOTHING LIKE LOVE

Love is an abstract thing used by soft people as something to take their minds off their work. If it were a concrete thing it would be too hard for most of us. You may cement friendships but concrete love is mortar-fying.

Some say love is a disease, but it's less of a disease than a complaint. No woman incapable of complaining ever gets married.

Ask any married man.

Love is a thing which gnaws into your bosom and then recommends a good brand of ointment and will bandage you up so you get worse.

The term 'He fell in love' is significant. He fell in—Love.

Men who fall deeply in love go off their meals. After they get married they go off for their meals. Love is Universal. It is just the same in Darlinghurst as it is in Oodnadatta, only in Darlinghurst it happens at shorter intervals.

Love-sick is a term generally applied to those in love. It shouldn't be.

Love makes the world go round. That's why it is flattened at both ends.

Love is to man a thing apart (and better that way), 'tis woman's whole existence (especially where the alimony is concerned).

There is nothing like love.

As for bargain sales—well, a husband is woman's most precious bargain. £ove! £ove! £ove!

SONG OF THE RAIN

HUGH MCCRAE

Night,
And the yellow pleasure of candle-light . . .
Old brown books and the kind fine face of the clock
Fogged in the veils of the fire—its cuddling tock.

The cat,
Greening her eyes on the flame-litten mat;
Wickedly wakeful she yawns at the rain
Bending the roses over the pane,
And a bird in my heart begins to sing
Over and over the same sweet thing—

Safe in the house with my boyhood's love,
And our children asleep in the attic above.

Australian author Colin Thiele sent the following letter to Rhonda Gill in July 1942,
on the eve of his departure from Adelaide to join the RAAF:

I remember when I first went to the University . . . I felt that I had
planned out a life for myself like the other undergraduates who were
reputed to be 'clever' and I came to believe that living and thinking as
related to myself were relatively simple matters if I only got down to
what were called 'basic principles' and stayed there.

And then I met you. I have never quite understood what processes,
emotional or otherwise, went on within me that day. The effect was
one which wrenched something in my soul. It was as if my emotional
life had been made of iron and was now suddenly placed within the
field of a gigantic electro-magnet. But the distortion was as subtle and
unexplainable as it was powerful and all-embracing . . .

I shall never forget you as you were on that first day: your pink dress,
your hair like bronzed gold, your blushing face as you became the
centre of everyone's attention. For me you will never ever be quite like
that again. Yet the amazing feature of it all is that until that moment
when I first met you my mind had not for a minute wandered from the
subject of the academic study I was making at the time. And even after
I had gone home and gone to bed that night you did not occupy my
mind at all explicitly. I really only became aware that something had

happened to me when I awoke the following morning. Just as one may fall asleep at night without thought of cold or chill and yet wake at dawn with a dry cough and rasping throat, so I awoke that morning with a positive though vague sense of pain somewhere, somehow, in my being. From that day, emotionally and psychologically, I began a new life. You became for me what no power had ever been before or is likely to be again. In Emily Bronte's words, 'You have gone through and through me like wine through water and altered the colour of my mind' . . .

It is all so strange and baffling, so dismaying, this parting. It cuts; it cuts deeply. A few months ago we would scarcely have entertained the idea; a few weeks ago we were regarding it as a distasteful shadow lying ahead; now it is upon us. I have been writing these words at night during the past weeks, often late after having seen you. And now that I must conclude this rather pitiful letter I am appalled by what is looming before us . . .

The very thought of parting from you, not in the vague future, not even in a few weeks, but within days and hours, accentuates the heavy dull ache I feel. And I believe that you feel it, too, perhaps more intensely than I. For you have so little to look forward to after I have gone. I shall have a few of my old friends with me, and I shall have new work, new sights, new experiences. You will have only your thoughts and recollections. Every day you must move about among the things that recall our laughing, working, talking, loving together, and they will be as bitter as gall. Some may say that *I* am making a sacrifice. But what is mine compared with yours? . . .

My heart aches when I think of you alone after I have gone. I yearn, how I yearn, to be able to stay with you always, in a world of quietness and understanding and peace; in a world of ordinary people and ordinary things—of books and study and daily life and love with you. And I vow to myself and to you that some day it shall be so . . .

All I can do is ask you helplessly, and without conviction, not to grieve more than you can help. Bear in mind that as you remember me, I am remembering you. As you read these words, I pray that you may see in them the picture of myself sitting as I am now, late at night, with my cheek resting on my hand, looking dully into blankness and thinking only of you. I trust that when I have gone these words, and the knowledge that I love you steadfastly and without reservation, may give you hope and courage, may sustain you in sorrow, and tide you over the great gulf of separation and spiritual loneliness that must be your lot. I know you are a true woman and as such will bite your lip in anguish and cover the sorrow in your heart.

Remember always that you have left your impress on me as surely as time itself. You have gone through and through me like wine through water. I will never forget you. You will be with me always—day by day, week by week, month by month. And some day, some day near or far, I will come back to you and then we shall drown all our sorrow and remorse, pain and heartburning, in a great rich and overflowing happiness.

'Goodbye, Rhonda'—yet even as you hear that, the time for our reunion is drawing closer and we move a moment nearer the time when I shall be packing my bag and coming back to you—when I shall be knocking on your door and asking for you. For never, as long as my heart beats and my eyes see, shall I forget you.

YOURS EVER,
COLIN

Colin and Rhonda were married in 1945 and enjoyed many years of happiness. On their fortieth wedding anniversary, Colin gave this poem to his wife:

FOR RHONNIE

We've climbed the world
in our own way,
the two of us together.
What an unforgettable journey!
Was it so long ago we made our choices,
contracted our futures, as the saying was?
Two people so fleetingly together
when moments had to be seized
and life was brittle under the roar of war.

But we survived,
and so began that partnership
rich with your presence.

You had no need of rhetoric,
assertiveness, squalling about rights,
or dolorosas over human roles.
As liberated as quicksilver
you were what you wanted to be.

Nothing could chain your spirit;
you knew how to be yourself.

And in that self was loyalty compounded,
kindliness, compassion and the fine hard grain
of unbudgeable conviction.

Were we to undertake our living
a second time
I think we would follow the same footsteps
as before.

So let's push forward then
to that last knoll
a little further on.
The view from there, they say, is infinite.

SADIE NORDEN WAS A JEWISH MILLINER WHEN XAVIER HERBERT MET HER
IN LONDON. HE WAS BROKE AND READY TO HOCK HIS TYPEWRITER FOR £6.
SMALL AND GENTLE, IT WAS SHE WHO LISTENED FASCINATED TO HIS STORIES,
TALKED HIM INTO WRITING *CAPRICORNIA* IN 1938 AND SUPPORTED HIM IN A
GARRET WHILE HE DID IT.
'DON'T GET THE IDEA,' HERBERT ONCE SAID, 'THAT SHE WAS SOME POOR
HUNGRY-HEARTED LITTLE CREATURE HARD UP FOR LOVE. SHE WAS AN
EXCEEDINGLY BEAUTIFUL GIRL, A JEWESS, WITH THE UNCANNY ASTUTENESS
OF HER RACE, AND SHE SAW UNDER MY HAIRY HIDE.' HE ADDED THAT HE
IDENTIFIED COMPLETELY WITH HENRY LAWSON'S 'BASTARD FROM THE
BUSH': ' "WOULD YOU LET A WOMAN KEEP YA, WOULD YOU GIVE UP WORK
FOR GOOD?" AND THE BASTARD FROM THE BUSH REPLIED: "MY BLOODY
OATH I WOULD".'
NOTWITHSTANDING ALL THE TOUGH TALK, IT IS TO SADIE THAT THE
MIGHTY *CAPRICORNIA* WAS DEDICATED.

HER SOLDIER
YVONNE WEBB (1940)

We have only a moment,
Hold me closely ere you go,
I hear the tramp of marching feet,
And time is fleeting so.
I'll knit you everything you need,
I'll write you every day,
And think about you constantly
The months that you're away.
I never will forget you,
Though you're far across the sea,
And I'll be waiting gaily here
When you return to me.

LOVE ME AND NEVER LEAVE ME

RONALD McCUAIG

Love me, and never leave me,
Love, nor ever deceive me,
And I shall always bless you
If I may undress you:
    This I heard a lover say
    To his sweetheart where they lay.

He, though he did undress her,
Did not always bless her;
She, though she would not leave him,
Often did deceive him;
    Yet they loved, and when they died
    They were buried side by side.

May Moore 1881–1931, Mina Moore 1882–1967, *Shirley Huxley*, c.1928

Kay Grant's doggerel was much prized by Australian troops during World War II and typifies the slangy good humour adopted in adverse times:

CO-OPERATION (1944)

When you meet the wench who shakes you, the perfect piece of skirt,
Who makes your backbone tremble and thrills run up your shirt,
Then sacrifice to all your Gods, give hostages to fate
And hope as man has ever hoped—that she'll co-operate.

You can dress with snap and smartness, you can even slick your hair,
You can cover up your knee-knobs and leave your biceps bare,
You can talk with utmost brilliance, your wit may scintillate,
But you can't get any further if she won't co-operate.

You can even join the army—how those leggings show your curves!
You can beg her with a quiver to restore your war-torn nerves,
You can always blame the Major if you find you're running late
But you can't get any further if she won't co-operate.

You can spend a fortnight's salary—buy her cigarettes, champagne,
You can call for her in taxis and take her home again.
You can use the 'Gable' clinches when you're parting at the gate,
But you can't get any further if she won't co-operate.

You can feed her quail and caviare (ie: Russian sturgeon)
And all the things just made to tempt the wise or foolish virgin.
You can offer her the moon and stars on a diamond-studded plate,
But you can't get any further if she won't co-operate.

You can have the usual breakdown—but don't get off your bike,
If she hands you out the frozen mitt and says she'd rather hike.
You can plead and say it's springtime, when even lizards mate,
But you can't get any further if she won't co-operate.

You can lure her to your parlour—you can even dim the light,
Think you've got her where you want her, and everything's just right.

Then she says she really *must* go home—it's getting *frightfully* late
You *can't* get any further if she won't co-operate.

You can think of all the books you've read, that told you—'treat 'em rough'
You can make a perfect swallow dive and try the cave-man stuff.
You may think you're getting somewhere, but the truth I'm bound to state,
You've two chances—mine and Buckley's—if she won't co-operate!

FORGETTING

*A poem by Sergeant-Pilot Bathurst
of the RAAF whilst stationed in
England during World War II.*

Forget you? Well, perhaps I may
Forget the very charming way
You smile, and then perhaps I might
Forget your eyes, your walk, your height.

Somehow, I even may forget
The way you hold a cigarette
So carelessly, and—who can tell?—
I may forget your voice as well.

With nonchalance, and sans regret,
All these things I might forget,
But the task too difficult to do
Would be forgetting—I love you!

Tarlton Rayment published a private collection of poems, Eagles and Earthlings, *in
1945 as a tribute to Australia's air crews. At the time, the bitter 'Drums of War' was
the focus of public attention; however, his wistful 'Incense of the Saplings' would also
have struck a chord with many homesick servicemen imagining the summer scent of
eucalyptus.*

Oh, come, my love, a-walking,
When the moon is young and pale;
When incense from the saplings
Makes for us a scented dale.

The brightest stars at even
are in your beloved eyes,
To set the leaves a-whispering
With flutterings and sighs.

The amethystine shades of night
drift down upon the breeze,
To paint fantastic silhouettes
Of gnarled and knotted trees.
When incense from the saplings
makes for us a scented dale,
O, come, my love, a-walking,
When the moon is young and pale.

John Kaufman 1864–1942, *Fairy Woods*

*There was a passing parade of romantic assignations when the American servicemen
came to Sydney during World War II. In this scene from Sumner Locke Eliot's* Edens
Lost, *Bea has been unable to enter the blacked out Royal Park Hotel to keep one
such date:*

She peered in, idiotically, through the chicken wire over Mark Foys'
windows, at sneering wax ladies wearing their wartime substitute outfits
furred in rabbit. She deliberated on the ladies preening in the unlit
shop windows because if she delayed long enough then on returning
perhaps the hotel door would be open, blazing with light. When, quite
nearby and startling, booming, she heard the clock in Town Hall strike
seven, she ran all three long streets back to the hotel to find it continuing
to sleep in darkness. She walked up and down thinking quite seriously
of the police being the only way she could get in. But the thought
of questions and answers handicapped her; the thought of breaking locks
and forcing entry with a cordon of police, paying for property damage,
a curious crowd watching, in order to keep an appointment with a
man she had not known till Friday evening held her back.

The fact that she could not walk away interested her. The fact that
she would keep up this cold vigil if necessary until midnight or until
he came out in order to prove to him that she had not let him down
interested her. It was a side of herself she did not know existed. All
she'd ever done was proclaim in lofty prose her feelings of passion
for the two other miserable and, now she came to think of it, puny
affairs. Now she was being called upon to perform a service of faith
. . .

And she was so impressed by this thought, so carried away, that
she found she had failed to notice a man and a woman coming out
of the Royal Park and screamed, wait, screamed across to them and
ran almost in front of a taxi. 'Stupid f'kin' sheilas,' the driver yelled
as she almost fell in the gutter. 'Don't shut the door,' she called.

'Oh, I want to get *in*,' she panted. 'I've been trying to get in for
two hours.'

'Are you expected?' the woman asked.

'Oh, yes, yes.'

'Then they'll come down and let you in if you're expected.'

'They—he—doesn't know I'm *here*,' she almost screamed. The man
and the woman looked dubious. 'Captain Orcutt. He's on the third
floor. He's *expecting* me,' she said, almost in tears. 'But he doesn't
know I'm *down* here.'

So, knowing everything now and with looks of sorrow reserved for
call girls, the man wordlessly took out a key. 'Tch, tch,' said the woman.

The lift ascended with the rapidity of treacle. Corey's face was as
unreceptive as the bell downstairs. He was pressed and polished, all

pink and American-eagle-gold-buttoned, parade-ground beautiful he was. She clutched at him untidily. 'Dear God,' she began, fell into the armchair and, because of the relief, became suddenly brilliantly amusing about it, pouring out the saga. How she went back and forth to the phone booth, how she stood and called and called. But he was either so glad or compassionate that he seemed not to find it amusing and finally cut her short quickly by saying in an exasperated way, 'There's an air transport going tonight and they put me on it.'

She shut her eyes for a moment; she'd noticed the bag on the bed.

'Oh, but *why*?'

'This is the Army, Mr Jones.'

'Oh, damn the Army to Hell and damn this frigging hotel and—' Why, she wanted to say, in Christ's name couldn't you have had the sense to see if someone was downstairs or look out the window or . . . But he looked so serious and stern that she knew not to say any of these things.

'What time do you have to go?'

'Have to report by twenty hundred hours—eight o'clock, in other words—but by the time I check out and find a cab . . . ' He scribbled a note while she tried to stop a hammering feeling in her own choked-down heart. Corey put his room key down on the note. Then she saw what he was doing was putting on his cap and picking up his valise and raincoat.

'Well?' he asked.

She hadn't thought he meant right now, this very second.

'Sure you have everything?'

'Think so.'

'Haven't left anything behind?'

She looked hopelessly in the empty wardrobe for him, peeped into the bathroom and then, as he was holding open the door with an air of impatience, she went with him obediently out of the room forever and he rang for the lift while she looked at a small hole in her glove. He made no move of comfort, no gesture of putting an arm around her; he looked on grey and stern beyond words as they crossed the lobby and he opened the front door for her. She had been inside, she reckoned, close to four and a half minutes.

As she walked beside him, she pretended to be busy straightening her belt so she might give an air of being impassive. He said nothing and she finally said huskily, 'Where are you going?'

'To Transport HQ in Bathurst Street.'

'Oh, *yes*,' she said, as though this were interesting.

They stood on the corner waiting for traffic to pass and he said nothing so she had to say it.

'Will you ever be back?'

'Oh, who knows? God knows. I have a hunch that the next trip will be to the States.'

'Yes. I see.'

'Who knows? If the war drags on another five years they might—on—hey, there's a cab! Better nab him. Taxi. *Taxi*.' They ran a few steps.

'Yes, well . . .'

'Well . . .'

'Take care of yourself.'

'You too.'

Then he said grimly, 'As far as anything goes, I still hold the record for perfect misses.'

'Oh, Corey.'

Then they kissed like relatives and shook hands at the same time. There were two American lieutenants in the cab. 'Going up Bathurst Street?' Corey asked. 'Hop in,' one of the Americans said.

He got in.

'So long, Bea,'

'Goodbye,' she said, but it was lost in the noise of the wheels.

Come in Spinner, by Dymphna Cusack and Florence James, created a ruckus when it was first published—albeit in an abridged version—in 1951 because of its descriptions of loosened morals in wartime Sydney. Pretty Guinea Malone has had her head turned by the flattery of American servicemen and only reluctantly accepts a date with her old sweetheart, Kim.

Guinea stretched out on the grass, her head touching his shoulder, her eyes on the blue sky that seemed to rest on the tall buildings framing the Square. A stunting bomber dived above the high arch of the Harbour Bridge and came in low over the park, swooping down with a roar. It zoomed up again in a silver flash. Three fighter planes plummeted out of the upper air to engage it in mock combat.

Kim blew a raspberry after the planes. 'Aw, go do your War Loan stunts somewhere else,' he admonished them. 'I'm off duty.' He turned to Guinea and his voice was urgent. 'Now, before those noisy cows come back again, will you . . .' the rest of his sentence was lost as another dive-bomber zoomed above York Street.

'What did you say?' Guinea shouted.

Kim moved closer and whispered against her ear. 'I said, will you marry me?'

She lay absolutely still. The grass was cool under her head, she could feel it short and springy against her bare legs. High up, the trails of the fighter planes were scrawled across the sky.

'I mean, it,' Kim whispered. He swore as he heard the rising roar of the returning bomber. 'Yes or no? Quick, Peg.' . . .

The poplar leaves turned over lazily in the breeze and she was filled with a deep sense of peace. Maybe it made her feel good to have Kim come crawling back to her at last. Maybe it was something else . . .

'Let's toss for it,' she said suddenly.

Kim sat up and looked down into her face; he was frowning and his mouth was set tight.

Why, she thought, I've never seen him look like that. He really means it. If he never meant anything before, he means this.

'I'm not very good at speeches, Peg. They're not in my line. But if you want any guarantee—you know, about being able to trust me and all that—well, for what it's worth, I've just quite suddenly wakened up to the fact that I could be the faithful kind.'

Her eyes met his and she looked at him for a long time. 'Give me someone worth being faithful to, and so could I.'

'I don't know if you feel that I come up to those specifications, but if you give me a chance I'll try to prove it.'

She stared up at him and then past him. The mock battle was still going on. Her mind followed the planes. If I marry you, she said to herself, then I'll never have any more peace. It'll start all over again. All the time you're away fighting, part of me will be there, too. I wonder if it's worth it . . .

'If it's love you're wanting me to talk about, Peg, I can turn that on, too.'

'I've heard you.'

'Then we'll skip it. Right now, what I'm asking you to do is to marry me—for keeps. Compared to what some of your other boyfriends can offer you, it mightn't seem much of a bargain to share my deferred pay when I come back and help to build up a rundown garage. But the way I see things, that's not all there is to it. It mightn't be easy, but it'll be fun and we'll be together and somehow, I can't think of anything better than spending the rest of my life with you.'

Guinea turned her face away. She wasn't sure she wanted any more of love. Not the kind of love she and Kim had had anyway. It hurt too much.

His voice was unsteady. 'You know, Peg, it suddenly struck me I'd rather like to have a kid like you. Maybe that's what all this love business really boils down to.'

Guinea's heart thumped. For keeps? And a kid of Kim's. She lay silent staring at the planes.

'Well,' he said at last, 'what's the answer?'

'Let's toss for it.' Her voice was clear and lazy.

He stared at her. She smiled back at him. There was a long pause.
'Do you mean that?'

'Huh-huh.'

'OK. If that's how you feel about it. But somehow, the way I look at it, it's a damned big thing to rest on the toss of a coin. But if that's the way you want it, I'd better find a brown.' He took a penny out of his pocket and tossed it experimentally. 'It's a new one if that's any help.'

'I hope it's not a double-header.'

'What a woman! You wouldn't trust anybody, would you?'

She looked at him without smiling. 'I might, you never know.'

'Well, here it goes.'

He spun the penny high in the sunshine and called 'Heads'. The lunchers near them turned to watch. It came down on the grass.

'Tails! Well, I can take it.'

Guinea looked at him, half smiling. 'You'd better have three tosses for luck.'

He flashed a quick glance at her. 'Whose? Mine or yours?'

'That depends.'

He tossed again. The conductor on a passing bus leaned out and bawled, 'Let the angels see 'em!'

'Heads!' Kim called again and it came down heads.

He rubbed the penny between his palms and spat on it. 'Now here goes for the lucky last.' It soared again, the new bronze sparkling in the sun. 'Heads!'

It landed between them—tails.

Guinea picked the penny up and looked at it, turning it over and over. Then she rubbed it between her palms, breathed on it and handed it back to him, putting her hands under her head and yawning with a pretence of unconcern. 'Maybe you'd better keep tossing until it comes right.'

Kim gave a whoop and all the heads turned round to look at them again. Uncle Sam quacked from the garden bed. Kim flicked the penny high in the air. 'There it goes,' he said, turning on his elbow and looking into her face. His hands closed over hers.

The new penny went up, spinning over and over against the blue sky. It came down on the edge of the garden, but neither of them bothered to look.

Writer David Malouf faced adolescence in Brisbane after World War II. His first love flickered—and waned—according to much simpler social customs that centred round ballroom dancing.

I had fallen heavily in my last year for a Somerville House girl called Roseanne Staples, who wore nylon stockings that shifted their lights like mother of pearl and was a G.P.S. diving champion. All one Wednesday at Moss's, and again the next, we danced dreamily under the rafters and I took her afterwards for mint juleps and malteds at the Pig 'n Whistle, a milk bar at the top of town that had been a favourite pick-up place for American soldiers and retained something of its wartime glamour and notoriety. It was regarded as daring and I was out to impress. When the waitress, who looked as if she might remember the place in the old days, slid our milk-shakes down the glass-topped counter, she winked in the direction of the innocent Roseanne and whispered: 'There y'are love. That'll put lead in yer pencil.' I could hardly wait for the week to pass. But on the third Wednesday, as we went whirling across the floor in what seemed to be a most accomplished manner, Roseanne, with a casualness that astonishes me even today, it was so low-keyed, so undramatic, pronounced the words that put an end to our affair, pfft! just like that, and changed the course of my life. Looking straight over my shoulder, in the most neutral tones: 'If there's one thing I can't stand,' said Roseanne Staples, slowly, 'it's boys who don't pivot.'

I was thunderstruck. The pivot—that little sidestep and pass at the corner of the floor that I had never quite got the knack of, it seemed so silly, hardly worth worrying about. I smiled wanly and guided her through the rest of the set, closing my eyes and swallowing hard as we approached the corners and wishing Moss's was triangular. *Four* corners was suddenly more than I could bear. Back safe among the boys I waited for something less subtle, like a Gipsy Tap . . .

Sydney—A Fine Town

Ronald McCuaig

Sydney is a fine town
And that's quite true,
And I love Sydney
Because I love you;

I love the long, crooked streets
The city through;
I've walked them all, side by side,
At all times, with you;

I love all the ferry-boats
That dance on the blue,
For I've gone a-voyagin'
In ferries with you;

I love all the theatres
And picture-shows, too;
You've kissed me in most of them
When I've kissed you;

But I don't love Shakespeare's
Bronze statue;
It was there that you left me
And I left you;

But I do love the alleyway
Where, in the 'Loo,
We both felt sorry,
As often we do.

Max Dupain b.1911–, *Rush Hour Kings Cross*, 1938

From The Sundowners

(1952) *by John Cleary*

'Paddy?' Ida said.

'Yeah?' He was sitting on the end of the mattress, taking off his boots. 'Got another hole in me sock.'

'Paddy, do I sound like a nagger sometimes?'

'Often.' Paddy had begun to cut his toenails, with a bone-handled penknife. 'Why?'

'Nothing.' Ida lay on the mattress that, spread on a large square of canvas, was their bed. She was naked beneath the thin grey blankets:

you realised the pointlessness of nightgowns when you had no money to buy one. Her long, dark brown hair lay in a wild splash beneath her head, and her tanned face, scrubbed just before she had got into bed, showed the bloom that had been hidden beneath the day's dust. She had long ago stopped admiring herself, but now and again, passing Paddy's shaving mirror hanging on the tentpole, she would stop herself for a moment, caught by a memory of sixteen years ago.

Camden had been the place, then, the only place, and she hadn't even been forty miles away to Sydney. Twenty, beautiful, some men had told her, and with a figure that was all the style then, all bosom and behind. Camden was a small town, and she had had a good time, and paid the penalty: gossip had trailed her like the wake of a ship. But she wouldn't have, couldn't have, changed. She had gone to church on Sundays, said her prayers, respected the Lord's Name, but the Lord had built her as she was. People could talk, but what was the whisper behind the hand to the whisper in your ear in the grass down by the river, the clucking of old women to the panting of a strong young man? Gossip was only envy, and she hadn't cared . . .

She stretched luxuriously under the blankets, stirred warmly by a memory that had only touch, no likeness or shape.

'What's the matter with you?' Paddy said, switching the penknife from his left to his right foot. 'Grinning like the cat that's swallowed the canary.'

'Wouldn't you like to know?' she said, but he was included in the smile and the memory.

The bells in the tower of the church on the hill chanting song on the still evening air; the tall gums stretching to the star-freckled blue; the river, whispering its way past them like an echo of the gossip; and Paddy, young and full of fire and blarney, only a week in the district and already in love with her and she with him. A wanderer even then, working on Bonney's farm only while the mood held him, then at the end of three weeks they were married and were gone. Just like that, while the town stood at its gates and said she had thrown herself away.

'But they were wrong,' she said.

'Eh?'

'Just talking to myself. Come on, for goodness' sake! Mucking about like an old woman.'

'I ain't any old woman. I can prove it.'

'That? I've seen bigger ones on statues. And they never have much.'

Naked, he was lean and hard-muscled as a man half his age. He patted his flat stomach. 'You're lucky, married to such a magnificent figure of a man.'

'Go on.' Ida waved a contemptuous hand. 'You're a midget alongside some of the men I used to know. Don't know what was the matter with me, marrying a little squirt like you.'

'You couldn't resist me winning ways.' Paddy blew out the lamp and slid under the blankets alongside her. 'Or me loving ways.'

Ida laughed scornfully. 'I had to teach you.'

Paddy ran a hand over her body, then let it rest on the firm plumpness of her breast. 'I'm glad you're built like you are, darl. Plenty of it. I was looking at some of them skinny flappers when we come through Kempsey—'

'Don't you ever let me catch you looking at any flappers. Or anything in skirts. I'll kick you in the you-know-where.'

'You wouldn't spoil your own fun.' He squeezed her breast and grinned at her in the dark. 'Yeah, I was looking at these young sheilas. Gawd, what does a man see in 'em? No tits or hips, a behind you could hold in one hand. A bloke might as well go to bed with a broomstick.'

'If you have to make a choice, you pick the broomstick. I'm warning you, my boy.'

'Do you really think I'd muck about with another woman, darl?'

'I don't know.' She turned towards him, her hand resting on the muscled hardness of him. 'When you're drunk and don't know what you're doing—'

'When I'm *that* drunk, I wanna go to sleep. I don't wanna get into bed for any other reason.'

'I love you, Paddy.' She pressed herself against him, holding him tightly while she kissed him as if to bind him to her forever. 'I couldn't stand to think of you with anyone else.'

'You ain't got to worry about that, darl.' His hand was stroking the soft thickness of hair at the back of her head. 'You're the only one. Always.'

In Ray Lawler's classic play, Summer of the Seventeenth Doll *(1957), Queensland cane-cutters visit their girlfriends in the city every summer during the 'lay-off' period. On this final trip, battle lines are drawn between Pearl, the 'respectable' widow, and Olive, desperate to defend her seventeen-year-long love affair with Roo:*

Olive: (in quick hostility, snapping off the radio) Now look, that's one thing I'm not gunna stand for. Right from the start!

Pearl: What?

Olive: You know what! That respectable mother stunt. Don't you try and put that over on me.

Pearl: I didn't say a word.

Olive: You said wrong, didn't yer? 'N' nasty mess? That's enough. I've told yer over 'n' over again what this lay off is, yet every

time you open yer mouth you make it sound like something—
low and dirty. Well, if that's the way you look at it, you
don't have to stay, y'know—nobody's forcin' you to make
any decisions about it—you can get your bags from the hall
and clear out before they get here.

Pearl: (defensively) Just because I don't think it's altogether proper.

Olive: Yeah. Just because of that.

Pearl: Nobody would say it was a decent way of living.

Olive: Wouldn't they? I would! I've rubbed shoulders with all sorts
from the time I was fourteen and I've never come across
anything more decent in my life. Decency is—it depends on
the people. And don't you say it doesn't!

Pearl: I meant decent like marriage. That's different, you said yourself
it was.

Olive: (with a slight shudder) It's different all right. Compared to all
the marriages I know, what I got is . . . (groping for depth
of expression) is five months of heaven every year. And it's
the same for them. Seven months they spend up there killin'
themselves in the cane season, and then they come down here
to live a little. That's what the lay-off is. Not just playing
around and spending a lot of money, but a time for livin'.
You think I haven't sized that up against what other women
have? I laugh at them every time they try to tell me. Even
waiting for Roo to come back is more exciting than anything
they've got . . .

*Elizabeth Lane grew up during the Depression on a farm in the Wimmera district of
Victoria. In her autobiography,* Mad as Rabbits, *she recalls spying, scrub style, on
her sister Marj's burgeoning romance:*

One Sunday when toothache had kept Ann home from the mushrooming
expedition, I turned back and followed Marj when we separated. Before
she'd gone very far, she turned and hurried into the scrub.

Nobody with any sense ever went mushrooming in scrub, so I
immediately grinned to myself. And when I saw a pimple-faced lad
who had attended every Salvation Army rally come out of the scrub
to meet her, I knew my suspicions were justified.

I made a detour around the paddock, and then, fencepost by fencepost,
bush by bush, I crept, stalked and wriggled until I was safely sheltered
in an umbrella-bush about ten yards from where they sat on a log at
the edge of the scrub.

I wished I had Ann there to giggle with me. The young man told
Marj she had the most beautiful eyes in the world; and she gazed into

F.A. Joyner 1863 1945, *Jack and Jill*

his face with wide-open eyes, not once referring to his pimples, which I felt was unfair, considering that she was forever throwing off at our boys about pimples . . .

When I heard him tell Marj that he would leave a note for her in the hollow of the big strainer-post on the corner of the paddock on Wednesday I nearly laughed out loud. Then I wriggled, crept and stalked, bush by bush, fencepost by fencepost, until I was back in the open paddock again. I was impatient to race home and tell Ann, but when Marj and I met in the open paddock, each innocently swinging an empty billy, I suddenly felt many years older than Ann and closer to Marj, and how glad I was that Marj did have the most beautiful eyes in the world . . .

All the same, this feeling of closeness to Marj didn't stop me from making a round trip past the hollow strainer-post on my way to school on Wednesday and lifting the promised note from it.

At playtime I took Renie Bryce into the seclusion of the wattle tree and showed her the letter.

'Eyes like stars! Lips ripe for love!' How we giggled over those tender passages.

I replaced the letter on the way home from school, but from the way Marj looked at me after that I knew she was aware I had discovered her romance.

That summer we still went mushrooming, even when it was no longer the season for mushrooms, Ann being outmanoeuvred before we left the house.

When we 'accidentally' met Pimple-face, who was also busy mushrooming out of season, I would leave them and—feeling I now knew all the intricacies of courting, and considering them rather silly— gladly wander off in the scrub and enjoy myself collecting different sorts of grubs and caterpillars, and eating wattle-gum, or lying on my back, hands pillowing my head, working out pictures in the different cloud-formations—whiling away a pleasant hour or two before rejoining Marj.

Dorothy Gordon Jenner, or 'Andrea', was much loved for the cheery 'Hello, Mums and Dads' that preceded her radio programmes on both 2GB and the ABC during the 1960s.

She described herself as lucky in love, but not in marriage. Her first husband drank some of his own wood alcohol and promptly died. She met her second at a suicide (!) and maintains 'the only good thing about him was that he had a tubercular testicle'.

Perhaps she would have been happier with Prime Minister Billy McMahon? Playboy Billy was 'all over me like a rash', said Andrea:

'When he asked me to marry him, I said "Oh, Billy, I'm always getting proposed to by the most improbable people. You might as well marry your grandmother!" I'm sure he's glad I refused because he's now very happily married to Sonia, who was only two years old at the time . . . I'm great friends with both of them and we often laugh over our little *amour*.'

God! How I Long for You

Kenneth Mackenzie

God! how I long for you, sealed up in night,
when in the lonely darkness of this bed
I lie awake with shut eyes, shut mind
enclosing your white image, shut ears
tormented by the echo of your voice.
This is not love. This is timeless torment—
a cruelty of the gods, who let you rob me
of my old easy unconsciousness of time,
and weight each second with your heavy memory—
each minute a thick coin stamped with your face,
each hour intolerable, each day a nightmare
of speechless, frightened, desperate anticipation,
and every night a sepulchre containing
my murdered body and your body's ghost.

PAS DE DEUX FOR LOVERS

MICHAEL DRANSFIELD

morning ought not
to be complex—
the sun is a seed
cast at dawn into the long
furrow of history

to wake
and go
would be so simple

yet

how the
first light
makes gold her hair

upon my arm.
how then
shall I leave
and where to go   day
is so deep already with involvement

A PRETTY ENGLISH GIRL I KNEW WAS BLUNTLY TOLD BY HER AUSTRALIAN
BOY-FRIEND THAT HE COULD NOT TAKE HER OUT ON FRIDAY NIGHT AS THAT
WAS THE NIGHT HE ALWAYS GOT DRUNK WITH THE BOYS.

JOHN DOUGLAS PRINGLE

Australian Accent (1958)

Max Dupain b.1911–, *Nude*, 1938

The adventures of Italian Nino Culotta on his arrival in Australia in 1964 prompted the entertaining They're a Weird Mob. *Called the funniest book about Australians ever written, it is also very warm and human, particularly the scene where the lonely migrant decides to pay court to an Aussie girl:*

I could see in my mind my house being built. I could see it standing amongst lawns and shrubs and flowers, with the bush behind it. I wanted to start. I wanted to get married. Joe put his hand on my shoulder and stood up. 'Hope she doesn't turn yer down, mate.'

I was remembering his words all the week. I did not want Kay to turn me down. I was sure now that I wanted her for my wife. I wanted her for my wife very much. But perhaps she would not want me. What had I to offer? I was a foreigner. No one of my blood was in this country. I was alone. I was proposing to ask her to marry a foreign bricklayer with no family. To live in a tent in the bush, whilst I cleared land and built a house. There would be metal and sand and brick-dust and cement and mess everywhere. What would her parents say to this? If she agreed, they would say she was mad. I was calmly proposing to ask this of a girl I had known only for a few weeks. I was certainly mad. I was frightened. I could not believe that she would agree, and yet I hoped she would. I could not sleep. I worked and I worried. I walked and prayed. I was no longer a man. I was inadequate. I was useless. I was a conceited fool.

I stepped off the ferry at Manly and saw Kay waiting for me. She was wearing a black suit, with an emerald green scarf at the throat and not a hat. She looked beautiful and dignified, and unapproachable. I wanted to get back on the ferry. I wanted to go home. To Italy. To my mother and my father and my sisters and my brothers, where I would not be lonely and useless and foreign. Now. When I was walking so slowly towards God's finest creation, whom I had dared to think could be my wife. Nino Culotta's wife. Nino Culotta who wasn't worthy even to touch her gloved fingertips. Nino Culotta who wished he was home with his mother. Should he jump into the water? It would be wet and cold and under the wharf it would be dark and he could hide amongst the piles. She was moving towards him. He looked at her shoes. They stopped in front of him. Her gloved hand touched his arm. He heard her voice. There was concern in it.

'Nino, what's the matter? Are you sick, Nino?'

'I am useless and foolish and conceited. You could not possibly marry a foreign bricklayer who has no family and only a tent to live in.'

The other gloved hand was under my chin, and pressing it up. 'Look at me,' she said. She smiled. 'Poor Nino. Nino, are you proposing to me? Here, amongst all these people?'

'I am very foolish. I wish to go home.'

'It was a bad week for me, too, Nino. I was afraid you wouldn't like me enough. And I wanted you to like me enough. Do you like me enough, Nino?'

I looked at her and could not answer. But I must have answered without words. She said softly, 'You and I are good for each other, Nino. I will be with you whenever you want me. And always . . . '

I could not speak. I could feel tears in my eyes. She put her hand under my arm. 'Let's walk,' she said. We walked all the way to the beach and neither of us said anything. We looked at the waves breaking in the cool sunshine. I found my lost voice again. I said, 'Kay, did you mean what you said? You will marry me?'

'You know I will,' she said. 'No more tears?'

'I am sorry about that.'

'I'm not. I'm glad I saw them. And I'm glad you didn't see mine last night. What was that about living in a tent?'

I told her my plan. She said, 'Dad won't like that. But I will. You can show me what to do and I'll help.'

Italy was a terrible place. Who would want to go back there? My parents would probably be horrified if I arrived home to stay. They liked to think of their brave son amongst the savage Australians. I would send them a picture of Kay. Perhaps one day I would take her home . . .

She interrupted my thoughts by saying, 'Tomorrow night you'll be having tea with my family. Scared?'

'Not now. Do I ask your father for his daughter's hand?'

'Good grief no. He'd die of shock. I'll tell him in the morning.'

'He will not die of shock then?'

'I think he knows. At least I think he's been hoping.'

'He need not worry. I will take care of you, Kay.'

'I know. I'm a very lucky girl.'

'How much costs an engagement ring?'

She laughed so much she could not eat. The Australian sense of humour is sometimes very difficult to understand. I still have trouble with it at times.

Articles and books on 'Strine', the Australian version of phonetic speech, captured the Aussie sense of humour in the mid-1960s. Here is 'Without You,' in Strine.

> With air chew, with air chew,
> Iker nardly liver there chew,
> An I dream a badger kisser snite and die
> Phoney wicked beer loan,
> Jar chewer mere non-air roan,
> An weed dreamer batter mooner pinner sky.

Pitching Woo

Charmian Clift

One of the prettiest girls I know is a red-head, Venetian red, with that particular translucent white skin that sometimes, but not always, goes with it, and cornflower eyes. She is a gentle, good-tempered, uncomplicated creature, but as gay and gregarious as a girl of her age should be, and without being avid for pleasure she loves dancing and parties and clothes and company. She has worked interstate for the adventure and experience, and presently rooms in a small flat with another girl of her own age. She is responsible and independent and deliciously attractive.

So when she told me that she had never once been taken out to dinner I was flabbergasted. And the more flabbergasted that she didn't seem to think such criminal neglect on the part of the male sex extraordinary in any way at all. With her peers and playmates apparently this is the normal behaviour pattern. There is a group, and the group frequents a discotheque, but the girls arrive independently, pay for their own drinks, leave independently too, unless someone with a car is going their way, or several of the group decide to make a party at somebody's flat or house. Couples pair off rather casually, some have even been known to progress as far as becoming engaged. And if I understood correctly her amused little dissertation on current tribal customs it would be possible within this behaviour pattern for a girl to achieve the state of matrimony without actually having been courted at all.

Mercy! No flowers, no candles, no personal table, personal corner, personal waiter paternally misty-eyed (the 'our place, remember darling?' of tender reminiscence on anniversaries years later), no park benches in the rain, no midnight vigils under an enchanted window, no agonies and ecstasies of quarrel and reconciliation, no despair over a mute telephone, no tokens, signs, passwords, favours, secrets? No foolish things? No banners, bugles, trumpets, tuckets, drums? No pale loitering? The pavements, one gathers, stay firmly fixed beneath this generation's feet, and mooning is for the birds, only not these birds.

Should one mourn the passing of the pitching of woo? Maybe this present level-headed camaraderie is really more sensible, the pay-for-yourself idea more realistic. Perhaps such a system is more in accord with a move towards sexual equality, and wooing as anachronistic to this lot as Victorian delicacies of courtship were to us.

Gone for ever now, excepting as nostalgic shades whirling around Bobby Limb, are a whole generation of navy-blue suits, the wooers who wore brilliantine to their wooing, and bought boxes of chocolates in the interval at the Saturday night pictures and gardenia sprays with maidenhair fern to grace their ladies' chiffon or morocain for the evenings of intoxicating fox-trotting. Gone the Sunday drive in the country, tea with the family, and afterwards the dark verandah where the fuchsias shielded the wicker lounge with the cretonne cushions.

Gone the ritual graduation of presents, the manicure set the brush-comb-and-mirror, the cut-crystal powder bowl, the toiletries scented with old English lavender, the blue satin bedroom mules racy with ostrich feathers, the penultimate commitment of the eighteen-jewel wristwatch and the tacit understanding that the ring came next.

Gone too the ardent wartime wooers, made reckless by a well-cut uniform, a full wallet, a brief leave, and the heroic aura of imminent peril. I'll be down to get you in a taxi honey, with a purple orchid for your pompadour and a silver chain for your ankle and six pairs of stockings I picked up from an American, and we're going to paint the town red, paint it pink, paint it yellow, paint it spotted and striped honey, we're going to dance all night and have champagne for breakfast and I'll keep the handkerchief with your lipstick on it under my paybook and over my heart until I come home to you you you.

What a perfectly splendid time that was for the pitching of woo, and what a wonderful variety of pitchers there was to choose from. Even the most timid men acquired style and dexterity with so much fervent practice and so much competition, and girls never had it so good. We collected eternal vows like beads for a wampum belt, and although most of these proved in the course of time to have been ephemeral, we had, as they say, our memories.

Personally I've always thought that poets have an edge on other chaps when it comes to real pitching. To begin with they do so enjoy it, which is essential to the game. I was discussing this with a poet one day and he confided to me (not at all boastfully) that tears had seldom failed him and poetry never, especially if there was blotted evidence of the tears on the poem, which ideally, he said, should be composed in the small hours of the morning and delivered, with one simple flower—like a daisy or a single jasmine blossom—under the beloved's door at dawn. He had had great success with vigils too. He said that you didn't actually have to stay up all night . . . it worked just as well if you took up your position on her doorstep just before her normal getting-up time. As long as you looked haggard and unshaven and she found you there sighing beside the milk bottles. He told me a lot of pitches, in fact, which left me rather thoughtful.

Of course a wooer doesn't have to actually write poetry to use it. The sonnets are eternally serviceable, and Marvell and Herrick and Lovelace and the rest churned out enough really first-rate woo to be re-usable for hundreds of years. So did John Donne. But I wonder, just in passing, whether Dowson would work still. Does any young man with hollow cheeks and haunted eyes still swear that he has been faithful in his fashion? No, perhaps not. Or is it middle-age that gives me the retrospective giggles?

Foreign languages are of some advantage to pitchers too. Even now I know girls who succumbed to the soft incomprehensibility of broken foreign phrases where the most plausible pleading in impeccable English had never even swayed them: sometimes, perhaps, it is better all round not to understand too well. And Continentals, like poets, play the game so well and so enjoy playing it that they can make poverty work better for them than big-time wine buying, and a bunch of field flowers do duty for two dozen perfect red roses.

Well, glory be! I suppose if you've never had it you don't miss it, and these young things will find their mates eventually without all the complicated rituals and heartaches and headaches and feastings and fastings that were so entrancing and absorbing, but, crikey, I'm glad I was young in the days when men pitched woo.

Robert McFarlane, Lovers, *Repins Cafe*, c.1963

SHE LOVES ME
DAVE UNDERWOOD

She loves,
She loves me not—
Hi!
She loves me,
Ooops,
She loves me not.
Great minds,
She loves me.
Clash, ideological change,
She loves me not.
Touching,
She loves me.
Fading image,
She loves me not.
Yearning,
She loves me.
Met,
She loves me not.
Tightly drawn, a need,
She loves me.
Old age—she loves me/
        she loves me not.

THE FEMALE EUNUCH (1970)
Germaine Greer

Love is . . . the drug which makes sexuality palatable in popular mythology.

Love, love, love—all the wretched cant of it, masking egotism, lust, masochism, fantasy under a mythology of sentimental postures, a welter of self-induced miseries and joys, blinding and masking the essential personalities in the frozen gestures of courtship, in the kissing and the dating and the desire, the compliments and the quarrels which vivify its barrenness.

137

WELSH-BORN BUILDER'S LABOURER PAUL DU FEU FELL HEAD OVER HEELS IN LOVE WITH GERMAINE GREER WHEN HE SAW HER WALKING IN LONDON'S PORTOBELLO ROAD ONE SUNNY SATURDAY IN 1968:

She was like a Dodge City gunfighter headed for a shoot-out, a strong intelligent face under a halo of brown hair. The sunshine was highlighting the extraordinary beauty of her brows and cheekbones and nose as her head tilted and pivoted. At one moment she was a pre-Raphaelite beauty, then a flick of her head transformed her into a wisecracking heroine of a 1930s movie.

A TUMULTUOUS ROMANCE RESULTED IN A MARRIAGE THAT ONLY LASTED THREE WEEKS; IN FACT, THEY STARTED FIGHTING TWO HOURS AFTER LEAVING THE REGISTRY OFFICE. DU FEU PROFESSED FEW REGRETS, PROMPTLY POSING NUDE FOR *PENTHOUSE* AND PENNING A BOOK ABOUT HIS EX-WIFE CALLED *LET'S HEAR IT FOR THE LONG-LEGGED GIRLS*.

THE LETTER
ELIZABETH RIDDELL

I take my pen in hand
    there was a meadow
    beside a field of oats, beside a wood,
    beside a road, beside a day spread out
    green at the edges, yellow at the heart.
    The dust lifted a little, a finger's breadth,
    the word of the wood pigeon travelled slow,
    a slow half-pace behind the tick of time.
To tell you I am well, and thinking of you
    and of the walk through the meadow, and of another walk
    along the neat piled ruin of the town
    under a pale heaven, empty of all but death
    and rain beginning. The river ran beside.

It has been a long time since I wrote. I have no news.
I put my head between my hands and hope
my heart will choke me. I put out my hand
to touch you and touch air. I turn to sleep
and find a nightmare, hollowness and fear.
And by the way, I have had no letter now
For eight weeks, it must be
a long eight weeks,
because you have nothing to say, nothing at all,
not even to record your emptiness
or guess what's to become of you, without love.
I know that you have cares,
ashes to shovel, broken glass to mend,
and many a cloth to patch before the sunset.
Write to me soon, and tell me how you are
if you still tremble, sweat and glower, still stretch
a hand for me at dusk, play me the tune,
show me the leaves and towers, the lamb, the rose.
Because I always wish to hear of you
and feel my heart swell and the blood run out
at the ungraceful syllable of your name
said through the scent of stocks, the little snore of fire,
the shoreless waves of symphony, the murmuring night.
I will end this letter now. I am yours with love.
Always with love, with love.

Robert McFarlane, *Helen Nude, Darlinghurst,* c.1977

SASSY

KATE LLEWELLYN

She screws up the pages
they write on in restaurants
as she doesn't want him to know
she wants to keep them

she strides in tall boots
very sassy
round the park
because she wants to keep him thinking
she doesn't care too much

when she's ill
she uses rouge and wine
so he can't tell

she has other lovers
so he won't guess
it's him she wants

she calls him Pisspot and Wild One
and hits him on the back
to keep him guessing
she flops in chairs
and sticks her boots out
so he won't see she's nervous

she drinks up and slams her glass down
so he won't see she's trembling

all in all it's a tremendous effort
and it doesn't fool him.

Robert McFarlane, *Mandy, Sydney*, c.1978

MEDITATION ON WYATT II

GWEN HARWOOD

'Forget not yet, forget not this'
  We are what darkness has become:
  two bodies bathed in saffron light
  disarmed by sudden distances
  pitched on the singing heights of time
  our skin aflame with eastern airs,
  changed beyond reason, but not rhyme.

'The which so long hath thee so loved'
>> counting the pulsebeats   foot to foot
>> our splendid metres   limb to limb
>> sweet assonance of tongue and tongue
>> figures of speech to speech   bemused
>> with metaphors as unimproved
>> as the crooked roads of genius

>> but our hearts' rhymes are absolute.

FROM LOVE POEMS

BOBBI SYKES

I
like the look of you/
moving easily in the street/
>> stopping to notice the clouds/
>>>> the flowers/
>>>> the cut-price clothes
in store windows;
Eyes slipping stealthily sideways
to catch your own image in the windows/
>>>> as you pass
to make sure you look
as good as you feel.

I noticed you yesterday/too/
>> and a time or two before that/
But then/
>> I was in haste/
>> doing my thing/
And you just flashed into my mind and vision
>>>> looking GOOD/
But today/
>> you look good/
>>>> and available.

Tracy Moffatt b.1960–, *Some lads 1*, 1986

DOMESTIC POEM
DOUGLAS STEWART

My wife, my life, my almost obligatory love,
Heaven forbid that I should seem your slave.
But perhaps I should say I saw you once in the garden
Rounding your arms to hold a most delicate burden
Of violets and lemons, and as you came up the path—
Dark hair, blue eyes, some dress that has got me beaten—
Noting no doubt as a painter their colour and shape
And bowing your face to their fragrance, the sweet and the sharp,
You were lit with delight that I have never forgotten.

When Puberty Blues *was published in 1979 it was greeted with shock and, in some quarters, revulsion for its decidedly bald portrayal of life in Sydney's southern suburbs. However, the raw rituals of adolescence remain familiar to many who grew up in the early 1970s, irrespective of suburb or city:*

Bruce Board was tall, blond and drove a panel van. He'd left school early, like some of the boys in the gang. He was a top guy, 'cause he had money, a car and a brand new board. Now all he needed was a brand new chick.

Bruce and I sauntered towards each other. The gang circled the chosen two, jeering and prodding.

'Go get 'er, Brew.'

'Kiss 'er, Boardie. Go on.' The ring closed in around us. My heart was thumping.

'Come on . . . We're waitin' . . . '

'Rip in Brew. Don't be shy . . . ' Sneer, snigger. This was it. He took me by the shoulders and we kissed.

'Yyyaaay.'

'Ooooh. Wooo.' Whistle.

'We're goin' for a walk,' he told me, leading me off to the bushes by the hand.

'It only takes ten minutes,' called out Strack after us. The boys roared with laughter.

Behind the lantana we kissed again.

'Will you go round wiv me?' he said.

And that was the courting ceremony in Sylvania Heights, where I grew up. Everyone was 'going around' with somebody. If a guy didn't have a girlfriend, he'd just pick one from a distance. Someone about his height, his hair colour, not too fat, not too skinny and always wearing a pair of straight-legged Levis . . .

Getting a friendship ring was the biggest thing in a girl's life. If you had a ring you were a top chick. Girls rushed up to you every day at school.

'Give us a look. Oh . . . is it 18-carat?'

'Yeah, have a look.'

'Oh gee he treats ya good. It's bewdiful.'

'Yeah he treats me roolly good and stuff.'

'How long have you been goin' round with 'im now?'

'Three months, two weeks, four days and um . . . what's the time? . . . two hours.'

'Whenja get it?'

'Saturday night.'

On the way home from your boyfriend's place, just after he'd given you a ring, you'd pause under the street light and examine it. Was it 18-carat? . . . Phew . . .

By day, we were at school learning logarithms but by night—in the back of cars, under the bowling alleys, on Cronulla Beach, down behind the Ace of Spades Hotel, in the changing rooms of the football field, or, if you were lucky, in a bed while someone's parents were out—you paid off your friendship ring.

SKY DIVE
JOAN HENDRY

Love at 40?

    How absurd!

Ask anyone from twenty-five . . .

To five.

A fire-cracker that fizzles

And goes out—

Says brutal Mayakovsky.

But Mayakovsky died

At thirty-five.

Absurd—

The way your smile

Lights up another
On my face
Without my willing it.
Absurd how beautiful
Each sparrow is,
How cherished
Every sickly city tree.
Absurd—
The eager way we walk
To meet each other
On the street.
Absurd the way the goddips fuss
When our casual glances—lock.
Absurd!
Absurd, endearing word
That dogs us everywhere we go
Till all the world is in the know
But us.
Now our fingers—accidentally—meet
And my heart tumbles
    30,000
      feet
And after such a dive
Is just as much alive
As I remember it
At twenty five.

The archetypal Good Bloke, A. B. Facey, set down his memoirs in A Fortunate Life. *Here he reminisces lovingly about his wife and the extraordinary coincidences surrounding their first meeting after World War I; and lovingly about her passing:*

A few days after the armistice we received some trench comfort parcels from home. Strange as it seems, I was the only person in my section to get socks; the others got all sorts of things, such as scarves, balaclavas, vests, notepaper, pencils, envelopes and handkerchieves. I found a note rolled up in my socks and it read: 'We wish the soldier that gets this parcel the best of luck and health and a safe return home to his loved ones when the war is over.' It was signed 'Evelyn Gibson, Hon. Secretary, Girl Guides, Bunbury, W.A.' A lot of my mates came from Bunbury

May Moore 1881–1931, Mina Moore 1882–1967, *Billy Chisholm* c.1910s

so I asked if any of them knew an Evelyn Gibson. They all knew her and said she was a good-looker and very smart, and that she came from a well-liked and respected family. I told them that she was mine and we all had an argument, in fun, about this girl and we all claimed her . . .

One day while on leave, I went to Perth with another soldier from the hospital. We were walking down Barrack Street in a northerly direction when we saw two girls coming towards us. We were in uniform and had our battalion colours showing on the arm near the shoulder. To our surprise the girls stopped us and one of them said, 'Please excuse us, you're returned men from the Eleventh Battalion, aren't you?' We replied that we were. Then one of the girls said, 'We are from Bunbury.' Addressing me she said 'You resemble a boy we know who enlisted from Bunbury.' I replied that I was with a lot of boys from Bunbury at Gallipoli and I mentioned several. Both girls knew the names that I had mentioned. I then asked the girl who had spoken to me her name. Now. What a shock I got. She said, 'My name is Evelyn Gibson.' Straight away my mind went back to the trenches at Gallipoli and the pair of socks and the note . . .

Although I had never had any real schooling I knew what the word providence meant and that here it was now. Evelyn was the most beautiful girl I had ever seen. I felt as if I had known her all my life. I was really overwhelmed but I managed to suggest that the four of us go and have a cup of tea and a sandwich and talk about the boys from Bunbury . . .

After that, Evelyn and I often met, and when I had to stay in hospital she used to visit me as often as she could. Evelyn and her friend would travel up to Perth on the Friday night Bunbury 'Rattler' and return again on the same on Saturday night. They would come and visit us in hospital. And that was how Evelyn and I started our courtship.

Sadly, Evelyn passed away in 1976.

She died at seven o'clock at night in my arms. We had been married for fifty-nine years, eleven months and twelve days. So on this day the loveliest and most beautiful woman left me. Evelyn had changed my life. I had had two lives, miles apart. Before we married, I was on my own. It was a lonely, solitary life—Evelyn changed that. After our marriage my life became something which was much more than just me . . . The loss of my lovely girl, my wife, has been a terrible shock to me.

Love slowly like a ship full of flowers

SIDNEY NOLAN

Poem 1947

LOVE
ROSALIND GILLESPIE

I wish I was golden
with big tits
to wrap about you

I'm small breasted
white skinned with freckles
and you love me?

Robert McFarlane, *Bea Nude,* 1978

Monte Luke, *Ebb Tide*, c.1928

FINISHED
KATE LLEWELLYN

There'll be no more
lying on your shoulder love
or listening for your car

there'll be no more
drinking on the verandah love
or eating roasted veal

there'll be no more
my legs around your neck love
and howling at the moon

there'll be no more
hits across my mouth love
and crawling on the floor

there'll be no more
smoking listening to you curse love
or smiling drinking more

there'll be no more
crying because you rage love
or dancing up your drive

there's no more
love love

. . . Look in my eyes!
The golden lover haunting the fringe of your dreams
Laughed and was gone and left you forlorn and angry . . .
Look in my eyes and be glad.

DOUGLAS ALEXANDER STEWART
The Golden Lover, sc. 4.

From Campaign

By Jean Bedford

We scandalised the waiters at Kinselas. 'Wanton behaviour,' said the nice fair one, with pursed lips. He'd often poured us out at three a.m. after rowdy drunken dinners, but no-one approved of love.

Then, near election day, at dinner, he said, 'I'm worried about your expectations.'

'I've got none. Really.' Just—let this go on.

'I can't handle it. It's my fault. I didn't mean to let it happen. It's dangerous and I can't go on with it.'

I knew about his girlfriend, of course, but she was in another city. I only wanted what we had, I wasn't interested in the rest.

'But to stop. So suddenly.'

'It happened suddenly.'

'Straight in, straight out?' I watched his impatience at my bitchiness.

'We can be mates still.'

'Can we?' I stared at him. 'Is this how you make *all* your friends?'

He stared back. 'No,' he said. 'No, it's not.'

I'd intended not to talk about it at all, to be gallant, give in gracefully. Now I had all sorts of pride, hurt, defensiveness struggling out of me. I'd had too much to drink, I was confused. I couldn't help trying to fight for myself. Even though I knew fighting for yourself is fucked, when the other has already left the field.

'I don't know,' I said, 'if I can be your friend.'

It gave me some satisfaction that this seemed to hurt him. He was tired, as usual. I really didn't want to hassle.

'Did you ever tell him you were in love with him?' Iris said. 'Perhaps that would have helped.'

'No,' I said. 'It would have made it worse. I think. I tried to cover myself in the end. I can't *make* him want me if he doesn't. I bloody wish I could, but.'

'Well, you can cry on my shoulder,' she said. 'It might not really be over.'

'No. It's over. And I don't feel like crying on shoulders.'

We're friends now, I suppose we always were. We sometimes send each other postcards with lighthearted messages. I cut out obscure newspaper paragraphs that I think will interest him and he sometimes rings just to say hello. When he is in the city we meet for drinks, buy each other lunches, sometimes dinner—but not often, because the night-time is dangerous and besides it is to spend with the one you love.

Every now and then we are both at one of Harry's lunches. I never think—this is where we met. We gossip, I ask about his work, he asks about mine. I try to amuse him, I show off and am illogical, animated. He doesn't seem to mind—he likes me. We're fond of each other. He is his reserved self and I like that. I like his eyes and the way the smile breaks in his dark tired face. I like his honesty and his clear mind. It's good to have a friend like him.

I wrote him a poem recently but I haven't sent it. It's meant to make him laugh. It goes: If you're ever free, To fall in love with me, Please can I be, The first to know?

I'm going to say on the postcard, if I send it, 'This is a line from a short story I once wrote.'

SOUNDINGS
DAVID CAMPBELL

The littler noises of love,
Catch of breath, half cry,
The brush of eyelashes,
Finger touch of hair,
Of blue-white places,
My slender love, my love
More rare than versus,
Tenderer.

The sea in a shell
Is louder than the decipherings
lip to lip of our love.

Your smell is the smell
of brown boronia.
I cry out then.
I take a bush to bed.

The pallid cuckoo makes
A little noise.
His first notes climb
Like early Nancy eyes.
He fills green stems with sap
As lovers wake.

The honeyeater lays
Eggs of faint rose.
Like little dawns
Her praises rise
And I put out a hand
The honeyeater's notes
Are warm and round

In your cupped breasts
Under the eaves
My swallows stir at rest.

PRESENT TENSE

DOROTHY AUCHTERLONIE

'Nothing can ever come of it,' he said.
—Outside the window, the white rose waved its head,
A late bird sang, insouciant, in the tree,
The sunset stained the river red.

'There is no future, none at all,' he said.
—She stretched her arms up from the tumbled bed:
'What future has the river or the rose?' said she,
'The bird's song is, and nothing comes of red.'

He held her as the river holds the red
Stain of sunset; as, when the bird has fled,
The tree holds the song. 'Listen,' said she,
'Bird, rose and sunlit water sing from this bed.'

ENDNOTES

The editor and publisher gratefully acknowledge the following sources and authors for items of commentary, biographical detail and anecdotal opinion. (These endnotes are numbered according to the page on which the reference occurs.)

1 3 The commentary regarding Lt Ralph Clark and his wife Betsey appears in *The Journal and letters of Lt Ralph Clark 1781–1792* (1981) edited by Paul G. Fidlon and R. J. Ryan.

3 The portrait and letter of Samuel Marsden comes from *Samuel Marsden, The Great Survivor* (1977) by A. T. Yarwood.

4 Paul Brunton describes his impressions of Captain Bligh after researching his book in *Awake, Bold Bligh!* (1989).

5 The details of Ann Flinders and the 'bonnet incident' come from *Petticoat Parade* (1965) by Denton Prout and Fred Feely.

6 For commentary regarding the affair and marriage of George and Elizabeth Bass see *Petticoat Parade* (1965) by Denton Prout and Fred Feely.

8 The information about Lachlan Macquarie's refusal to take his second wife to India is part of Lysbeth Cohen's *Elizabeth Macquarie, Her Life and Times* (1979).

11 The description of John Macarthur's reliance upon and high esteem of his wife Elizabeth are taken from *Some Early Records of the Macarthurs of Camden* (1914) by Sibylla Macarthur-Onslow and *Australian Pioneer Women* (1982) by Eve Pownall.

11 Portia Robinson outlines the limited correspondence between convicts and the partners they left behind in England in *The Women of Botany Bay* (1988).

12 The description and details about the Female Factory, the type of 'speech' the officer-in-charge was recorded as having said to the assembled convicts when choosing a wife, and comments about the future of these marriages comes from *Petticoat Parade* (1965) by Denton Prout and Fred Feely.

14 Patricia Clarke reveals the separation of Thomas Braidwood Wilson from his wife Jane and the biographical details of them both in *The Life and Times of a Colonial Woman, Mary Braidwood Mowle* (1986).

15 16 Michael Langley gives his opinion on Charles Sturt's personality and how his feelings for his wife grew over time in *Sturt of the Murray* (1969).

19 For inference about the possible importance of Lucy Nicholson as a romantic interest for Ludwig Leichhardt see *Leichhardt the Dauntless Explorer* (1988) edited by Colin Roderick.

19 20 Jane de Falbe's inferred commentary about the possible romance between Ludwig Leichhardt and Emmeline Macarthur appears in *My Dear Miss Macarthur* (1988).

20 The story about Collit's Inn was derived from *The Fettered and the Free* (1987) by Iris Nesdale.

21 The comment and interpretation on Charles Harpur's nature, political expertise and biographical details comes from *The Poetical Works of Charles Harpur* (1984) edited by E. Perkins.

21 For biographical details about David Blair and Annie Grant see *Colonial Voices* (1989) by E. Webby.

24 Maggie Weidenhofer tells of Sophy Taylor's adventurous trip to Adelaide and what this trip would have meant to her friends in England in *Colonial Ladies* (1985).

30 31 The descriptions of Eureka Stockade, how school mistress Alicia Dunne hid and nursed Peter Lalor and their eventual marriage and land purchase in Ballarat are taken from *Famous Australians* (1983) by M. Hetherington.

32 The letter attributed to Janet Brown, sent to Frank Gardiner was first mentioned in *The Devil's Nightcap*, a novel by Lancelot Booth (NSW Bookstore Coy 1912). This letter and comments about Janet and Frank's real life exploits were found in *Petticoat Parade* (1965) by Denton Prout and Fred Feely.

33 34 Details concerning the experiences of convict William Sykes and his wife Myra and the life they lead in England appear in Alexandra Hasluck's *Unwilling Emigrants*.

34 For details about Henry Kendall's relationship with Rose Bennett and commentary on the way the poet took the end of the affair see *The Poetical Works of Henry Kendall* edited by T. T. Reed.

36 38 The information on E. W. Cole's advertisement for a wife, the response he received from Eliza Frances Jordan and the outcome of their meeting comes from *Ratbags* (1979) by Keith Dunstan.

46 47 Patrick O'Farrell is the editor of *Letters From Irish Australia 1825–1929* (1984), the book which gives the commentary and biographical

details about Alexander Crawford and his cousin Lillie and their eventual marriage.

51-53 The comments concerning the relationship between Mary Gilmore and Henry Lawson and inference about their possible romantic connection appear in *Poet of the Colours* (1988) edited by John Phillips.

55-57 The experiences of Patrick MacMahon Glynn as a parliamentary speaker and details of his relationship with Abigail Dynon is recounted in *Patrick MacMahon Glynn: Letters to his Family (1874–1927)* (1974), by Gerald Glynn O'Collins.

75 Peter Luck's *Bicentennial Minutes* (1988) is the source for the comments about Lottie Lyell and Raymond Longford and how they were buried together.

77 For commentary about Dorothea MacKellar's supposed love affair and presumed virginity see *My Heart, My Country — The Story Of Dorothea MacKellar* (1989) by Adrienne Howley.

92-93 The comment about Perth Ladies Sphere and May Gibbs is found in *May Gibbs — Mother of the Gumnuts* (1985) by Maureen Walsh.

94 Mary Gilmore's biographical details of her subsequent marriage and information concerning publisher A. G. Stephens' removal of the dedication to her in John Shaw Neilson's 'Her Eyes Foretold of Happiness', are from *Poet of the Colours* (1988) edited by John Phillips.

95 For the description of the meeting of Percy Grainger and Ella Strom and their subsequent relationship see Keith Dunstan's *Ratbags* (1979).

100 Kate White describes how Joe and Enid Lyons met, their feelings for each other and their biographical details in *A Political Love Story: Joe and Enid Lyons* (1987).

101 Kylie Tennant reveals the impressions of her youth and biographical details in her book, *The Missing Heir* (1986).

101 The description of Sidney Kidman's feelings for his wife are found in *Sidney Kidman: The Cattle King* (1936) by Ion L. Idriess.

102 The biographical information on Henry Handel Richardson comes from the two sources; *Australia's Writers* (1980) by Graeme Kinross Smith and *The Australian Dictionary of Biography* (1988) edited by Geoffrey Serle, Vol. 11 1891–1939.

103 The information in the introduction to 'Night of Romance' was derived from *Backless Betty From Bondi* (1983) by Kenneth Slessor and Virgil O'Reilly.

106 The description of W. C. Wentworth, his courtship of Barbara Baird and his propensity for unconventional telephone usage was taken from *Ratbags* (1979) by Keith Dunstan.

106 For reference to Lennie Lower's nickname for his wife Phyllis see *Here's Lower* (1983) edited by Tom Thompson.

110 Xavier Herbert's description, the interpretation of his comments about his wife Sadie and reference to Henry Lawson's sayings appear in *Ratbags* (1979) by Keith Dunstan.

128 The description of Dorothy Gordon Jenner's first husband, her opinion of him and her relationship with Billy MacMahon come from *Andrea — Darlings, I've Had A Ball!* (1975) by Trish Sheppard.

133 Peter Luck's *Bicentennial Minutes* (1988) gives a description of strine and how it achieved its place in the Australian language.

138 The comments by Paul De Feu about Germaine Greer were found in Keith Dunstan's *Ratbags* (1979).

ACKNOWLEDGMENTS

DOCUMENTS

Auchterlonie, Dorothy, 'Present Tense', *The Penguin Book of Australian Women Poets*, Hampton, Susan & Llewellyn, Kate (eds.), Penguin Books, Ringwood, 1986.

Australian Etiquette (1885), 'Love Letter, The' (Anon), *The Australian Womens' Diary 1986*, Doubleday Australia, Sydney, 1985.

Baxter, Annie, excerpts from *Memories of the Past by a Lady in Australia* cited in *Colonial Ladies*, Weidenhofer, Maggie (ed.), Currey O'Neill Ross Pty Ltd, Melbourne, 1985.

Bedford, Jean, from the short story 'Campaign', *Colouring In: A Book of Ideologically Unsound Love Stories*, Bedford, Jean & Creswell, Rosemary, McPhee Gribble Publishers, Melbourne, 1986.

Blair, David, letter to Annie Grant, *Colonial Voices*, E. Webby (ed.), University of Queensland Press, St Lucia, 1989.

Brennan, Christopher, 'Because She Would Ask Me Why I Love Her', 'I Am Shut Out Of Mine Own Heart', *Christopher Brennan*, Stumm, Terry, University of Queensland Press, St Lucia, 1984.

Broken Years, The, Letters of servicemen during World War I, Gammage, Bill (ed.), Australian National University Press, Canberra, 1974.

Brown, Janet, letter to Frank Gardiner, *The Devil's Nightcap*, Booth, Lancelot, NSW Bookstore Company, 1912.

Bruce, Mary Grant, *Billabong's Daughter*, Ward Lock, Sydney, 1924. Copyright c/- Curtis Brown (Aust.) Pty Limited.

Brunton, Paul, *Awake Old Bligh!*, Allen & Unwin/State Library of NSW, Sydney, 1989.

Campbell, David, 'Soundings', *David Campbell: Collected Poems*, Angus & Robertson, Sydney, 1989. Copyright c/- Curtis Brown (Aust.) Pty Limited.

Cassee, Pierre, 'The Shearer's Serenade', *The Penguin Book of Humorous Verse*, Scott, Bill (ed.), Penguin Books, Ringwood, 1984.

Clark, Lt Ralph, excerpts regarding his wife Betsey, *The Journal and Letters of Lt Ralph Clark* 1787–1792, Fidlon, Paul G. & Ryan, R. J., Australian Documents Library, 1981.

Cleary, Jon, *The Sundowners*, Fontana, London, 1968.

Clift, Charmian, 'Pitching Woo', *The World of Charmian Clift*, William Collins, Sydney, 1983.

Crawford, Alexander, letter to Lillie Matthews, *Letters from Irish Australia* 1825–1929, O'Farrell, Patrick (ed.), NSW University Press, Sydney & The Ulster Historical Foundation, 1984.

Culotta, Nino, *They're a Weird Mob*, John O'Grady Classics, Ure Smith Press, Sydney, 1964.

Curlewis, Herbert, letter to Ethel Turner, *The Diaries of Ethel Turner*, Poole, Philippa, Ure Smith Press, 1979.

Cusack, Dymphna & James, Florence, *Come in Spinner*, Angus & Robertson, Sydney, 1988. Copyright c/- Curtis Brown (Aust.) Pty Limited.

Dawson, Keith, anecdotes and biographical excerpts on Xavier Herbert, E. W. Cole, Percy Grainger and Charles Wentworth, *Ratbags*, Golden Press, 1979.

De Feu, Paul, *Let's Hear it From the Long-legged Girls*. Copyright Anthony Sheil Assoc. Ltd, London.

Dennis, C. J., 'The Play', *Poets of Australia*, Halstead Press Pty Ltd, Sydney, 1946.

Dransfield, Michael, 'Pas de Deux for Lovers', *Michael Dransfield: Collected Poems*, Rodney Hall (ed.), University of Queensland Press, 1987.

Eliot, Sumner Locke, *Eden's Lost*, Michael Joseph, London, 1946. Copyright Sumner Locke Eliot 1969.

Facey, A. B., *A Fortunate Life*, Penguin Books, Ringwood, 1986.

Feely, Fred & Prout, Denton, letters concerning Matthew & Ann Flinders, *Petticoat Parade*, Rigby Ltd, Adelaide, 1965.

Fowler, Frank, *Southern Lights and Shadows*, 1859, facsimile edition, Sydney University Press, Sydney, 1975.

Franklin, Miles, *My Brilliant Career*, Angus & Robertson, Sydney, 1901. Copyright The Miles Franklin Estate.

Gibbs, May, letter to Angus & Robertson, *May Gibbs — Mother of the Gumnuts*, Walsh, Maureen, Angus & Robertson, 1985. Copyright c/- Curtis Brown (Aust) Pty Limited.

Gillespie, Rosalind, 'Love', *Mother I'm Rooted*, Jennings, Kate (ed.), Outback Press Pty Ltd, Vic., 1975

Gilmore, Mary, 'To You', 'You-A-Wanting Me', *Mary Gilmore: Selected Verse*, Angus & Robertson, Sydney, 1948. Copyright The Estate of Dame Mary Gilmore 1948.

Gilmore, Mary, letter to Henry Lawson, *Poet of the Colours — the life of John Shaw Neilson*, Phillips, John (ed.), Allen & Unwin, Sydney, 1988. Copyright Public Trustee as executor of the Will of Dame Mary Gilmore.

Glynn, Patrick MacMahon, letters to his mother and Abigail Dynon, *Patrick MacMahon Glynn: Letters to his Family (1874–1927)*, O'Collins, Gerald Glynn, The Polding Press, Melbourne, 1974.

Godbyr, Josiah, excerpts from letters to his wife Rebecca, *The Women of Botany Bay*, Robinson, Portia, Macquarie Library, NSW, 1988.

Grainger, Percy, excerpts from letters. Copyright Grainger Museum, University of Melbourne.

Grant, Kay, 'Co-operation', *It's 'Ard To Go Wrong in the Suburbs*, Halstead Press Pty Ltd, Sydney, 1944.

Greer, Germaine, *The Female Eunuch*, HarperCollins Publishers Limited, 1971.

Harford, Lesbia, 'The Electric Tram to Kew', 'Love is not Love', 'Red Hat', *The Poems of Lesbia Harford*, Modjeska, Drusilla & Pizer, Marjorie (eds.), Angus & Robertson, Sydney, 1985.

Harpur, Charles, 'The Consummation', *The Poetical Works of Charles Harpur*, Perkins, E. (ed.), Angus & Robertson, Sydney, 1984.

Harwood, Gwen, 'Meditation on Wyatt II', *Gwen Harwood: Selected Poems*, Angus & Robertson, Sydney, 1975. Copyright Gwen Harwood 1990

Hepplethwaite, James, 'An Echo', *Picnics and Pleasures*, MacKenzie, Valerie, Centennial Publications, Sydney, 1982.

Hendry, Joan, 'Sky Dive', *Mother I'm Rooted*, Jennings, Kate (ed.), Outback Press Pty Ltd, Vic., 1975.

Herbert, Xavier, *Capricornia*, Lloyd O'Neill, Vic., 1971. Copyright c/- Curtis Brown (Aust.) Pty Limited.

Hill, Ernestine, *My Love Must Wait*, Angus & Robertson, Sydney, 1941.

Kelaher, Tip, 'Coogee Bay', *The Digger Hat and other Verses*, The Currawong Publishing Company, Sydney, 1942.

Kendall, Henry, 'At Nightfall', *Henry Kendall*, Wilde, W. H., G. K. Hall & Co., Boston, 1976.

Kendall, Henry, 'Rose Lorraine', *The Poetical Works of Henry Kendall*, Reed, T. (ed.), Libraries Board of South Australia, 1966.

Lalor, Peter, letter to Alicia Dunne, *Famous Australians*, Hetherington, Molly, Hutchinson Group, Richmond, 1983.

Lane, Elizabeth, *Mad As Rabbits*, Rigby Ltd, Adelaide, 1962. Copyright c/- Curtis Brown (Aust.) Pty Limited.

Langley, Michael, excerpts from letters, *Sturt of the Murray*, Robert Hale & Company, London, 1969.

Lauder, Afferbeck, 'Without You', *Let Stalk Strine*, Ure Smith Press, Sydney, 1965.

Lawler, Ray, *Summer of the Seventeenth Doll*, 1978. The permission of Currency Press, Sydney, to reproduce this extract from *The Summer of the Seventeenth Doll* is gratefully acknowledged.

Lawson, Henry, 'The Drover's Sweetheart', 'The Sliprail and the Spur', *Selected Poems of Henry Lawson*, Angus & Robertson, 1986.

Leichhardt, Ludwig, letter, *My Dear Miss Macarthur*, Falbe, Jane de (ed.), Kangaroo Press, Sydney, 1988.

Leichhardt, Ludwig, diary entry concerning Lucy Nicholson, *Leichhardt the Dauntless Explorer*, Roderick, Colin, Angus & Robertson, Sydney, 1988.

Lette, Kathy & Carey, Gabrielle, *Puberty Blues*, McPhee Gribble, Melbourne, 1979.

Llewellyn, Kate, 'Finished', 'Sassy', *Trader Kate and the Elephants*, Friendly Street Poets, Adelaide, 1979.

Louisa Anne Meredith, 'The Convict Woman' (Anon), Ellis, Vivienne Rae, Hobart, 1979.

Lower, Lennie, 'Nothing Like Love', *Here's Lower*, Thompson, Tom (ed.), Hale & Iremonger, Sydney, 1983.

Lyons, Joe, letter to his wife Enid, *A Political Love Story: Joe and Enid Lyons*, White, Kate, Penguin Books, Ringwood, 1987.

Macarthur, John, letters to his wife Elizabeth, *Some Early Records of the Macarthurs of Camden*, Macarthur, Sibylla, Sydney, 1914, *Australian Pioneer Women*, Pownall, Eve, Rigby Press, Sydney, 1982.

McCrae, Hugh, 'Song of the Rain', *Hugh Macrae*, Stewart, D., Angus & Robertson, Sydney, 1966. Copyright The descendants of Hugh McCrae.

McCuaig, Ronald, 'Love Me And Never Leave Me', 'Sydney — A Fine Town', *The Ballad of Bloodthirsty Bessie*, Angus & Robertson, Sydney, 1961. Copyright Ronald McCuaig 1961.

Mack, Louise, *Teens Triumphant*, P. R. Stephenson & Co, Sydney, 1933.

MacKellar, Dorothy, 'Looking Forward', *The Poems of Dorothy MacKellar*, Dredge, C. K. & Elkins, B. K., Rigby Ltd, 1971. Copyright c/- Curtis Brown (Aust.) Pty Limited.

MacKenzie, Kenneth, 'God! How I Long for You', *Selected Poems of Kenneth MacKenzie*, Angus & Robertson, Sydney, 1961. Copyright E. Little and H. MacKenzie 1972.

Macquarie, Lachlan, excerpt from diary MS#C.T. 73 & 74, The Mitchell Library, State Library of NSW.

Macquarie, Lachlan, journal entry, *Elizabeth Macquarie, Her Life and Times*, Cohen, Lysbeth, National Library of Australia, Canberra, 1979.

Malouf, David, reminiscence, *Australian Autobiography*, Colmer, John & Colmer, Dorothy, Penguin Books, Ringwood, 1987.

Marsden, Samuel, letter of proposal, *Samuel Marsden, The Great Survivor*, Yarwood, A. T., Melbourne University Press, Melbourne, 1977.

Meredith, Louisa, excerpt from *My Home in Tasmania* cited in *Colonial Eve — Sources on Women in Australia*, Teale, Ruth, Oxford University Press, Melbourne, 1978.

Moore, Tom Inglis, 'To My Wife', *Poets of Australia*, Halstead Press Pty Ltd, Sydney, 1946. Copyright Estate of Tom Inglis Moore.

Morant, Harry 'The Breaker', 'The Good Things That Remain', *Breaker Morant*, Cutlack, F. M., Ure Smith Press, Sydney, 1962.

——, 'A-Shelling Peas', *The Poetry of Breaker Morant*, McNicholl, David, Golden Press, Sydney, 1980.

Neilsen, John Shaw, 'Her Eyes Foretold of Happiness', *Poet of the Colours — The Life of John Shaw Neilsen*, Phillips, John (ed.), Allen & Unwin, Sydney, 1988.

Nesdale, Iris, story about Collit's Inn, *The Fettered and the Free*, Orchid Publications, Adelaide, 1987.

New Oxford Book of Australian Verse, The, 'The Banks of the Condamine', 'The Lass in the Female Factory' (Anon), Murray, Les A. (ed.), Oxford University Press, Melbourne, 1987.

Ogilvie, Will H., 'His Gippsland Girl', 'A Tell Tale Tryst', *Poems of Will H. Ogilvie*, Angus & Robertson, Sydney, 1958. Copyright G. T. A. Ogilvie 1952.

Oodgeroo of the tribe Noonuccal, custodian of the land Minjerribah, 'Gifts', *The Dawn is at Hand*, Jacaranda Press, Brisbane, 1966.

Paterson, A. B., 'As Long As Your Eyes are Blue', *Singer of the Bush — A. B. Paterson Complete Works 1885–1900*, Campbell, E. R., Landsdowne Press, Sydney, 1983. Copyright Retusa Pty Limited 1921.

Prichard, Katharine Susannah, 'Love Philtre', *Poets of Australia*, Halstead Press Pty Ltd, Sydney, 1946. Copyright c/- Curtis Brown (Aust.) Pty Limited.

Prichard, Katharine Susannah, *Coonardoo*, Angus & Robertson, Sydney, 1929. Copyright c/- Curtis Brown (Aust.) Pty Limited.

Pringle, John Douglas, *Australian Accent*, Chatto & Windus, London, 1958.

Quinn, Roderic, 'Just To Drift', *Poems*, Angus & Robertson, Sydney, 1964. Copyright Noreen Quinn 1920.

Rayment, Tarltong, 'Incense of the Saplings', *Eagles and Earthlings*, Wartime Production, no publisher, 1945.

Richardson, Henry Handel, *The Fortunes of Richard Mahoney*, William Heinemann Ltd, 1917.

Riddell, Elizabeth, 'The Letter', *From the Midnight Courtyard*, Angus & Robertson, Sydney, 1989.

Rudd, Steele, 'Sarah's Courtship', *On Our Selection*, Australian Classics Giant, Lloyd O'Neill, Hawthorne, 1973.

Sheppard, Trish, *Andrea — Darlings, I've had a Ball!*, Ure Smith Press, Sydney, 1975.

Slessor, Kenneth, 'A Night of Romance', *Backless Betty from Bondi*, Slessor, Kenneth & O'Reilly, Virgil, Angus & Robertson, Sydney, 1983

Stewart, Douglas, 'Domestic Poem', *A Feast For St Joseph*, (the last unpublished poems), *Garden of Friends*, Viking, Ringwood, 1987. Copyright c/- Curtis Brown (Aust.) Pty Limited.

Stone, Louis, 'The Courting of Pinkey', *Jonah*, Angus & Robertson, Sydney, 1981.

Sykes, Bobby, 'Love Poems', *Love Poems and Other Revolutionary Actions*, University of Queensland Press, St Lucia, 1988.

Sykes, Myra, letters to her husband William, *Unwilling Emigrants*, Hasluck, Alexandra, Oxford University Press, Melbourne, 1959.

Taylor, Irene C., excerpts from *Sophy Under Sail* cited in Colonial Ladies, Weidenhofer, Maggie (ed.), Currey O'Neill Ross Pty Ltd, Melbourne, 1985

Tennant, Kylie, *The Missing Heir*, Macmillan Company, Melbourne, 1986. Copyright c/- Curtis Brown (Aust.) Pty Limited.

Thiele, Colin, excerpt of letter to his fiancée Rhonda Gill. Copyright Colin & Rhonda Thiele.

——, excerpt of letter written to his wife Rhonda on their fortieth wedding anniversary. Copyright Colin & Rhonda Thiele.

Throssell, Ric, excerpts and poem about Katharine Susannah Prichard and her husband Jim Throssell, *Wild Weeds and Windflowers*, Angus & Robertson, Sydney, 1990

Underwood, Dave, 'She Loves Me', *Dimensions*, Dawe, Bruce (ed.), McGraw Hill, Sydney, 1974.

Webb, Yvonne, 'Her Soldier', *The Australian Women's Weekly*, Sydney, 1940.

Wilson, Thomas Braidwood, letter to his wife Jane, *The Life and Times of a Colonial Woman: Mary Braidwood Mowle*, Clarke, Patricia, Allen & Unwin, Sydney, 1986.

ILLUSTRATIONS

(These acknowledgments are numbered according to the page on which the illustration occurs)

(iii) *Glimpse of a Bedroom*, c. 1930, At Work and Play Series, 'Girgarrie', Vic, The Mitchell Library, State Library of NSW, Small Picture File (SPF).

1   Joseph Fowles (c. 1817–1878), *Ship in Full Sail Passing Sydney Heads*, c. 1840, oil on canvas; 45 x 61 cm, Rex Nan Kivell Collection, National Library of Australia.

2   John Vine Hall, *Sydney Harbour Islands*, 1863, Sketches of Sydney Collection, The Mitchell Library, State Library of NSW, SPF.

4   Drawn by J. Russell, engraved by H. Adlard, *Governor Bligh*, from Rev. T.B. Murray's Pitcairn, 3rd ed. London, 1854, The Mitchell Library, State Library of NSW, SPF.

7   *Matthew Flinders*, 1801, min. portrait, watercolour on ivory (framed with end of hair at back). From the original drawing in The Mitchell Library, State Library of NSW 1991.

8   *The Bedroom at Old Government House*, Parramatta, c. 1924, National Trust of Australia (NSW Branch).

9   *Australian Aborigines — Dwellings*, The Mitchell Library, State Library of NSW, SPF.

10 Bill ('King Billy') Barak, *Native Tribal Scene with Australian Native Animals*, c. 1870s, watercolour and pencil on paper stuck to card, sheet and comp; 56.6 x 78.8 cm, not signed, not dated. Gift of Mrs A. Fraser, 1934, Ballarat Fine Art Gallery.

12 *The Female Factory at Parramatta*, built c. 1820, The Mitchell Library, State Library of NSW, SPF.

15 Eugene Von Guerard (1811–1901), *Murray River, Moorundi* 1867, hand col. lithograph; 32.5 x 51 cm, Eugene Von Guerard's Australian Landscapes, plate No. 18, National Library of Australia.

18 Untitled illustration, *Bulletin*, 9 Dec 1899, Peter Luck Productions.

20 William Hetzer (1857–1879), *Portrait of G.L. Onslow*, photograph from the Macarthur Family Album, The Mitchell Library, State Library of NSW, SPF.

23 Charles Arnold, *'I can't work today'*, 1900, Actors and Actresses Series, The Mitchell Library, State Library of NSW, SPF.

27 *The Sick Stockrider*, a still from the 1913 film, National Film and Sound Archives.

28 *Portrait of a Young Girl with Roses*, from Daniel O'Keefe's Australian Family Album (1982), The Mitchell Library, State Library of NSW, SPF.

31 William Macleod, *Peter Lalor* 1886–1888, The Mitchell Library, State Library of NSW, SPF.

32 *Bushrangers Holding Up Coach*, c. late 1800s, Bushranger and Bushranging Series, The Mitchell Library, State Library of NSW, SPF.

33 *Leg-irons dug up at Williamstown*, Vic, 1902, The Mitchell Library, State Library of NSW, SPF.

34 William Strutt (1825–1915), *Gold Diggers Receiving a Letter from Home*, c. 1860, oil on canvas; 91.5 x 72.3 cm, purchasing 1964, Art Gallery of NSW.

35 E. Garfield Andrews, *At Nightfall*, c. 1910, photograph used in *Australia: Image of a Nation* by David Moore, permission granted by Edward Andrews.

37 *Cole of the Book Arcade*, cover from the book of the same name — a biography of E. W. Cole by Cole Turnley, The Mitchell Library, State Library of NSW, SPF.

38 Irene Brown, Australia (1898–1984), *Portrait of a woman writing*, 1940, gelatin silver photograph; 14.6 x 11.0 cm. Gift of Miss Irene Brown 1981, Australian National Gallery.

40 Harold Cazneaux, Australia (1878–1953), *The Veil, Blue Mountains*, National Library of Australia, permission granted by Rainbow Johnston.

42 Frederick McCubbin, Australia (1855–1917), *Home Again*, 1884, oil on canvas; 85.0 x 123 cm, purchased through the Art Foundation of Victoria with funds provided by G. J. Cole Pty Ltd 1981, National Gallery of Victoria.

43 *A Man Reading a Letter*, 1890s, The Mitchell Library, State Library of NSW.

45 *Arrival of the Mailman*, Kerry photograph, Powerhouse Museum.

47 *A Man and his Dog*, c. 1890, Western Australia, The Mitchell Library, State Library of NSW.

49 *Miss Ethel Turner (Mrs Curlewis) and her Daughter*, Alba photo, Sydney, The Mitchell Library, State Library of NSW, SPF.

50 *Mary Gilmore*, photograph, The Mitchell Library, State Library of NSW, SPF.

52 *Henry Lawson* c. 1910, photograph, The Mitchell Library, State Library of NSW, SPF.

53 Percy Leason, *Henry Lawson Selected Poems*, 1918 edition of the book, woodcut cover illustration, The Mitchell Library, State Library of NSW, SPF.

55 *New South Wales Parliament, Legislative Council*, 1895, The Mitchell Library, State Library of NSW, SPF.

59 David Davies (1864–1939), *From A Distant Land*, 1889, oil on canvas; 80.9 x 115.6cm, purchased 1968, Art Gallery of NSW.

62 *Dad and Dave Come to Town*, Peter Luck Productions.

65 *Alexander Ryrie and his sister Evelyn of Michelago Station*, Cooma District, Kerry photograph, Powerhouse Museum.

67 *Pioneer's Wife*, Kerry Photograph, reg. no. 930, Powerhouse Museum.

71 Frederick McCubbin, *The Little Housewife* (1905–1910), oil on composite board; 23.8 x 34.0cm, The Ewing Collection, The University of Melbourne Art Collection.

72 J. W. Lindt (1845–1926), *Gossip*, Fernshaw, 1882, albumen print in Album 13, Australian Scenery, National Library of Australia.

77 Harold Cazneaux, Australia (1878–1953), *Winifred Cazneaux*, 1906, gelatin silver photograph; 9.7 x 7.3cm, Gift of the Cazneaux family 1981, Australian National Gallery, permission granted by Rainbow Johnston.

79 Unknown photographer, *Portrait of Dorothy MacKellar*, c. 1915, presented to The Mitchell Library by Mrs J. Rutledge, The Mitchell Library, State Library of NSW, SPF.

80 L. Hey Sharp, Australia (1885–1965), *Melbourne*, 1929, bromoil photograph; 15.8 x 11.4cm, Australian National Gallery.

85 *Shakespeare*, c. 1920s, Actors and Actresses Series, The Mitchell Library, State Library of NSW, SPF.

86 *Wayside Letterbox*, c. 1920s, The Mitchell Library, State Library of NSW, SPF.

89 *The Old Wharf, Mosman Bay*, c. 1920, laminated photograph, The Mitchell Library, State Library of NSW, SPF.

90 *Billabong Daughter*, cover illustration from the book by Mary Grant Bruce, The Mitchell Library, State Library of NSW, SPF.

93 Jack Kilgour, *Portrait of Nancy Kilgour*, 1932, oil, The Mitchell Library, State Library of NSW.

95 *Portrait of Ella Strom*, The Mitchell Library, State Library of NSW, SPF.

96 Sydney Long (1871–1955), *By Tranquil Waters*, 1894, oil on canvas; 11.1 x 183.7cm, purchased 1894, Art Gallery of NSW.

99 Frank H. Johnston, *Aboriginal Stockman*, Bedford Downs Station, Kimberleys, WA, National Library of Australia.

102 *Henry Handel Richardson* (1870–1946), photograph by Elliot and Fry, London c. 1940, The Mitchell Library, State Library of NSW, PC27.

104 *Diggaburra*, The Digger Tea Supply Co. Qld, 1922, from *Symbols of Australia* by Mimmo Cozzolino & G. Fysh Rutherford.

105 Adrian Feint, *The Jetties, Palm Beach*, 1942, Gift of Howard Hinton, The Howard Hinton Collection, New England Regional Art Museum, Armidale, NSW.

111 *Relatives and Friends Farewelling the Strathallen off to War*, Australian War Memorial.

112 May Moore (1881–1931), Mina Moore (1882–1967), *Shirley Huxley*, c. 1928, gelatin silver photograph; 15.0 x 20.5cm, May and Mina Moore Collection, La Trobe Library, State Library of Victoria.

115 John Kaufman (1878–1953), *Fairy Woods*, brown carbon photograph; 21.2 x 29.6cm, Gift of John Bilney 1979, Art Gallery of NSW.

121 *Sydney Mail Cover*, 29 July 1931, black white and red, The Mitchell Library, State Library of NSW, SPF.

123 Max Dupain (1911–   ), *Rush Hour Kings Cross*, 1938, Max Dupain Studio.

127 F.A. Joyner, Australia (1863–1945), *Jack and Jill*, gelatin silver photograph; 42.3 x 36.0cm, Gift of Mrs Max Joyner 1981, Art Gallery of South Australia.

129 *Lonely Interior*, 1939, Adelaide, At Work and Play Series, The Mitchell Library, State Library of NSW, SPF.

131 Max Dupain (1911–   ), *Nude*, 1938, Max Dupain Studio.

136 Robert McFarlane, *Lovers, Repins Cafe*, c. 1963.

139 Robert McFarlane, Helen Nude, Darlinghurst, c. 1977.

141 Robert McFarlane, *Mandy, Sydney*, c. 1978.

143 Tracey Moffatt, Australia (1960–   ), *Some Lads I*. 1986, gelatin silver photograph; 45.5 x 46.5cm, Kodak (Australasia) Pty Ltd Fund 1987, Australian National Gallery.

144 Jeff Carter, *Spectators At Yamba*, from p50 of *Surf Beaches of Australia's East Coast*, Angus & Robertson, 1968.

147 May Moore (1881–1931), Mina Moore (1882–1967), *Billy Chisholm*, c. 1910s, May and Mina Moore Collection, La Trobe Library, State Library of Victoria.

149 Robert McFarlane, *Bea Nude*, 1978.

150 Monte Luke, *Ebb Tide*, c. 1928, bromoil.

BIBLIOGRAPHY

Adelaide, Debra, *A Bright Fiery Troop — Australian Women Writers of the Nineteenth Century*, Penguin Books, Ringwood, Vic., 1988.

Barnard, Majorie, *The Persimmon Tree and Other Stories*, Virago Modern Classics, London, 1985.

Chapman, Peter (ed.), *Diaries and Letters of G. T. W. Boyes*, Oxford University Press, Melbourne, Vic., 1985.

Clark, Manning, *In Search of Henry Lawson*, Macmillan Company, Melbourne, Vic., 1978.

Donkin, Nancy, *The Women Were There*, Collins Dove, Melbourne, Vic., 1988.

Dutton, Geoffrey, *The Australian Heroes*, Angus & Robertson, Sydney, NSW, 1981.

Eldershaw, M. Barnard, *A House is Built*, Lloyd O'Neill, Hawthorne, Vic., 1972.

Frost, Lucy, *No Place for a Nervous Lady*, McPhee Gribble, Melbourne, Vic., 1985.

Howley, Adrienne, *My Heart, My Country — The Story of Dorothea MacKellar*, University of Queensland Press, St Lucia, Qld, 1989.

Hutton, Geoffery, *Adam Lindsay Gordon — the man and the myth*, Faber & Faber, London, 1978.

Idriess, Ion L., *Cattle King*, Angus and Robertson, Sydney, NSW, 1936.

Keesing, Nancy & Stewart, Douglas (eds.), *Australian Bush Ballads*, Lloyd O'Neill, Hawthorne, Vic., 1955.

Mangan, Kathleen, *Autumn Memories*, Georgian House, Melbourne, Vic., 1985.

Moore, John, *The First Fleet Marines*, University of Queensland Press, St Lucia, Vic., 1987.

Nance, Lindsay, *Prime Ministers of Australia*, Bison Books, London, 1989.

One Hundred Famous Australian Lives, Paul Hamlyn, Sydney, NSW, 1969.

Scott, Margaret, *The Black Swans*, Angus & Robertson, Sydney, NSW, 1988.

Spender, Lynne (ed.), *On Her Selection — Writings by Nineteenth-Century Australian Women*, Penguin Books, Melbourne, Vic., 1988.

Stewart, Douglas (ed.), *Australia Fair*, Ure Smith Press/Paul Hamlyn, Sydney, NSW, 1974.

Stone, Walter (ed.), *Poems of Henry Lawson*, Ure Smith Press, Sydney, NSW, 1973.

Vries-Evans, S. De, *Pioneer Women, Pioneer Land*, Angus & Robertson, Sydney, NSW, 1987.

Webby, E. & Wevers, L. (eds.), *Goodbye to Romance*, Allen & Unwin, Auckland, New Zealand, 1989.